M
OF T

DATE DUE		
OCT 0 4 2009		
SEP 0 2 2010		

Master
of the Music

Geneva Hiebert

MASTER OF THE MUSIC
Copyright © 2009 Geneva M. Hiebert

ISBN-10: 1-897373-68-6
ISBN-13: 978-1-897373-68-2

All rights reserved. No part of this publication may be reproduced, stored in a retrieval system, or transmitted in any form or by any means—electronic, mechanical, photocopying, recording, or any other—except for brief quotations in printed reviews, without the prior written consent of the copyright owner or publisher. Any unauthorized publication is an infringement of the copyright law.

This book is a work of fiction. Names, characters, places, and incidents are the product of the author's imagination or are used fictitiously. Any resemblance to actual events, locales, or persons, living or dead, is coincidental.

Published by Word Alive Press

131 Cordite Road, Winnipeg, Manitoba, R3W 1S1
www.wordalivepress.ca

To Bethany and Erin:

I hope that you'll always know

the wonder of His love.

Prologue   ix

The Gathering   1

Marcus   7

Catherine   25

Timothy   53

Marie   61

Joshua   75

Twila   105

Prologue

IT DRIFTED OVER THE LAND like a lazy river, winding over hills and meadows, lingering in the treetops like the clinging morning mist floating low over still waters. It mingled with the songs of the birds and was lost in the clatter of industry only to emerge again in the star-studded night. It wooed, whispering in the stillness of the moon and in the quiet of the woods; calling, ever calling; pressing and urging; gentle, patient and eternally persistent.

"Come away, come away…"

It called constantly and persuasively, "Come away from your life and into something gloriously new." Most heard the song at least once in a quiet moment but ignored its call. Many never again noticed the sweet strain, so intent were they on their own business. Sometimes, though, one would stop working, lift his head as he caught the sound, and then, after listening for a while, leave whatever he was doing to follow the call of the music.

Throughout the land messengers rode, calling attention to the song. "Have you heard it?" they would ask, "Have you heard the music? It is the call of the Master of all music. He is calling you to his land: a land full of beauty, song, and heroes. He is calling you to a land that is everything that means home. Come away and escape from the death of your lives. Come away! Can you not hear the music?"

Everywhere they went people scoffed at them and turned their backs, except for the few whose imaginations were captivated enough for them to take the time to listen. Once heard, the music became an irresistible draw, pulling its listener onward to the home of the Master. It was forever calling, forever tugging, leading the way; and step by step the distance would be covered, the obstacles overcome and the gates of the castle gained.

The road was never easy. It was filled with great snares and pitfalls set up by the enemy of the music; yet there was always rescue for those who truly heard the song. It drew them relentlessly out of the deepest pits and the most hopeless places. Sometimes they would cry out for help and rescue would come, wearing the armour of the Master's castle and mounted on magnificent horses. These were the servants of the Master, sent to destroy the enemy's work and help those following the music. These were the great knights who were trained and armed for battle after making their own journeys out of the world. Great battles were fought and not a single person who wanted to be found was ever lost. Yet the enemy and his servants persisted and tried to trick all who belonged to the Master or followed his song into betraying him. And so, great stories were born and new songs were sung as the Master and his warriors gathered all who would come and live for the music.

The Gathering

A LARGE LOG CRACKLED cheerfully in the enormous fireplace at one end of the castle library. Outside, the first storm of winter howled and beat miserably against the windows hung with heavy dark drapes that were drawn tight, as if to keep the storm at bay. The walls were lined to the vaulted ceilings with the thousands of books that made up the Master's collection, including several rare and ancient volumes that could be reached only by climbing one of the wheeled wooden ladders that ran on tracks around the room. It smelled of old leather, paper, and ink that had lasted for hundreds of years. There were a couple of scattered desks and chairs for working at, but it was too dark for that just then. A large overstuffed brown leather sofa flanked by a couple of cherry red leather wing chairs made an inviting vignette around the fire. It was a good place to spend a stormy evening sipping a cup of hot tea and staring, mesmerized, into the flickering flames.

The three who had found their way to the chairs assembled around the fireplace were enjoying the novelty of winter coziness. By spring they would be longing for the freedom of the outdoors, but tonight they revelled in being comfortably sheltered from the storm outside. They were an oddly assorted group, having wandered in singly and then remained, quietly sharing the experience with each other.

Timothy, older than the others and grey haired, with his gnarled, work worn hands permanently stained with earth, sat in one of the reading chairs. He had moved it a little bit away from the group so that he sat predominantly in the shadows. Nodding and listening more than he talked, he was content to puff very occasionally on his pipe and observe the others.

Marie, as headmistress of the girl's dormitory and one of the teachers at the school, occupied one end of the oversized sofa that directly faced the large open fireplace. She had the strength and beauty of a woman fully confident that she was in the right time and place in her life. A jagged scar that ran across one side of her face did nothing to mar her features, but rather, added more interest to a face that, if anything, tended to be more austere than she would have liked.

Twila, one of the students in her charge, quietly deferred to the older woman from where she sat on the opposite end of the couch. She tried to leave the comfortable spot when Marie first joined them, but when the headmistress made it clear that there was no need for her to go, she reluctantly stayed where she was out of the fear of appearing rude. She had, however, a disappointing sense that the teacher's presence meant the evening would be reduced to a mundane exchange of stilted commonalities. Her pale, slender face, framed by a sooty mass of black hair, still held traces of remembered pain. As her thoughts drifted, her expression reflected her emotions as transparently as a pane of glass. She was still relatively new to the castle and, in her own way, feared Marie's authority as she had learned to fear previous authorities in her life. She gazed thoughtfully into the fire and spoke only when spoken to, studiously making only the most expected of replies. It wasn't long before the conversation flagged and the three, running out of things to say to each other, fell into silence as they allowed their thoughts to drift.

Nobody really noticed at first when the door quietly opened and the Master walked in. Timothy was the first to see him coming and his eyes gleamed brightly as he smiled his welcome. Marie made a little more room for him on the sofa and patted the space between her and Twila eagerly in invitation. Twila, lost in her own reflection, didn't notice him until he sat beside her, then she eagerly linked her arm through his and leaned her head on his shoulder.

"I'm so glad you're here," she said, quietly joyful.

Perhaps the evening wasn't going be so dull after all. The two of them had been working closely together on a special project and she had seen a great deal of him, but it was a different and rare thing to just sit and enjoy a visit.

"This is a comfortable way to spend an evening," he said after they were all settled again.

"We've been listening to that wind and thinking about how much nicer it is to be in here," Marie replied.

"A good night for sharing stories, perhaps?" he suggested.

Twila squeezed his arm eagerly, "Oh yes! Please tell us a story."

The Master laughed a little and looked down into the eyes that were slowly regaining their childhood. It was a good thing that she had found her way to the castle when she did. For some, their childhood was lost forever.

"Well," he smiled tenderly into her eager face, "what would you like to hear about?"

"Tell us about the knights and their adventures," Twila answered quickly.

"All of them?" he teased her and then nodded thoughtfully and looked at the others. "Well, there was the time that Marcus was lost..." he began, then paused for a moment, as if in hesitation.

Timothy chuckled softly, eyes twinkling in understanding as they met the Master's when Twila—the little girl now bright in her—urged him on with a breathless, "How could that have happened?"

Before he could continue, the door opened again. They all turned to see a tall man enter the room and look around awkwardly for a moment, as if unsure of whether he should come any further. He had the uncomfortable air of somebody who would much rather have been outside and active instead of cooped up indoors by the storm.

"Well, why don't we let him tell you his own story?" the Master said in a voice loud enough to be heard by the newcomer. "Marcus, we were just talking about you. Won't you come in and join us? I was going to tell about the time you were lost in the fog, but since you're here, I'm sure you can tell it better than I could."

"There's just enough room for one more," Marie said persuasively, and she waved toward the last vacant chair opposite Timothy.

The big man moved carefully, as if he were afraid of knocking something over. He finally folded himself into the chair and grinned, happy at having found a safe resting place.

"I was just wondering what I was going to do with the rest of my evening," he said. "I'm not sure I'm better at telling this story, though. I've heard your version and it's pretty good, but I'll give it a try. I'm sure glad I'm not out there tonight," he commented as an especially forceful gust of wind rattled the windows. "Of course, the day I got lost the weather was beautiful. You couldn't have asked for a better June day, right up to the evening that is…"

Marcus

I SET OUT THAT MORNING with the Master's blessing ringing in my ears and in my heart. The patrol was routine and I headed for home that evening with nothing of significance to report. As I neared the castle, though, a fog set in, thicker and denser than anything I have ever seen before or since. I swear that I could not see the ears of my horse in front of me and even sounds became muffled and distorted so that the bell that calls us all to the dining hall suddenly seemed to come from everywhere at once and nowhere at all.

In retrospect, the wisest course of action would have been for me to stay exactly where I was until the mist cleared away and I could see where I was going. Yet, how often do any of us choose the wisest course of action when it means taking no action at all? After pausing for a few minutes to try to discover any clue about the way I should go, I turned my horse's head in the way that seemed best to me, although even now I'm not sure that I could give any real reason for choosing that way instead of another. The fact is that I simply couldn't stand to sit still. After all, a knight in the Master's service, a man of valour and action, must be decisive and sure at all times, isn't that right?

The horse went reluctantly, and in my frustration at being so uncertain of my way, I whipped him sharply until he made his way, trembling, but without anymore hesitation at least. I am still ashamed of that whipping, knowing now, as perhaps I guessed then, that the poor beast would have found his own way back to his stable if I had let him follow his own nose. If the idea had occurred to me, I probably would have dismissed it for the glory of feeling that I found my own way out of the predicament without depending on an animal to save me.

As it was, we continued on in the direction of my choice, with the horse snorting and trembling at every step until I whipped him again, for he was starting to inspire my own mind with doubts and fears. We made our way slowly, and as we advanced, it seemed to me that the sound of the castle bell became stronger and more clear. I realized that the Master must be having the bell rung to call any of us who might have trouble finding our way in the fog. I was greatly relieved that we had not wandered blindly into danger in the fog, although I wouldn't have admitted that at the time. Shortly afterwards, the shadow of the walls loomed before us, and although we had approached the rear of the castle, it would be a simple thing to follow the wall around to the gate.

"There, you stupid beast," I said triumphantly to the horse, "Here we are, safe and sound after all in spite of all your fear and trembling."

I have never really believed that animals can understand very much of what we say to them, but the words were no sooner out of my mouth than that crazy horse gave a great snort, promptly threw me off into a thorny hedge, and galloped away in the opposite direction. I remember grumbling angrily as I pulled myself out of the bushes and started on the long walk around the castle. A trip that would have taken a few minutes on horseback was going to take a least an hour of hard work, plodding around the walls in my heavy armour. I spent the time plotting all the things I was going to do to my rebellious mount to make him pay for my missed dinner.

After what seemed much longer than just an hour, I finally approached the front gate and eagerly picked up my pace as I began to anticipate the dry clothes and hot food that were waiting for me. I was suddenly struck by the silence. The ringing bell had long since stopped, and I supposed that the usual sounds of life behind the walls were muffled by the fog, making it seem unnaturally quiet. I was even more amazed when I crossed the drawbridge without a challenge from the guards that were usually stationed there. In fact, I did not see anyone at all standing guard and thought that this was very unusual, but then I remembered that sometimes the Master gives orders that seem odd to us at the time but ended up being better than if things went the ordinary way. There must have been someone there to open the gate, which swung silently open as I approached, even though I couldn't see anybody there. It swung closed behind me just as silently and I found myself in the castle courtyard, which, to my surprise, was just as full of people as usual. Still, nobody spoke to me, or anybody else, for that matter.

I watched as those around me went about their work, busy and intent on their various occupations, all maintaining absolute silence. In fact, not even a single head was raised as I slowly walked toward the front doors of the castle, my armour clanking obnoxiously in the quiet. I finally saw a familiar face and turned aside to approach him with a cheerful greeting on my lips and the obvious questions about what was going on just ready to burst out.

He looked up at the sound of my voice and I thought that his smile seemed to be tempered with just a touch of fear. He glanced around quickly, as if to check if any of the others were watching us, and placed a finger over his lips with a shake of his head. Everyone seemed to be ignoring us, even though I must have drawn a certain amount of attention just by being the only source of noise in the courtyard.

"What's going on?" I asked quietly.

"Shhhh," he warned me and shook his head at me again. Then, with a sigh, he softly whispered, "It's against the rules."

Finally I thought I understood. We were under special orders to maintain silence, so I nodded and smiled in reply, hoping to reassure him that I wouldn't say anything more. It had been a long time since we had seen each other and I was eager to find out where he had been and what he had been doing. But as things were, I decided that we would have to catch up another time. My stomach rumbled audibly and I decided that it would be better to go straight to my room and change out of my armour.

The sense of strangeness struck me even more strongly when I went inside. The long hallways that were usually so bright, airy, and decorated with rich simplicity were hung with heavy, elaborate tapestries that blocked the smallest breath of air, making them feel close and stuffy. Scented tapers hung at intervals and flickered dimly in the dark corridors. Initially, the combination of perfume and smoke was overwhelming—even nauseating—but after a while I became used to it and didn't notice it as much. The tapestries themselves were beautiful and I found myself pausing to gaze in awe at scenes from many of the stories I had heard told in the castle from the day I first entered. I was inspired as I passed picture after picture showing the great deeds of the Master and sometimes his followers. It was amazing how much things were changed after only a single day's absence, but I had learned long ago that the Master can accomplish extraordinary things, so I did not think to question what I saw.

At first I thought I had become disoriented in the redecorated halls, for my room was not where I expected it to be. I wandered along for a long time without any success and finally decided to seek out the Master himself and ask him what was going on. With this in mind, I turned my steps to follow the halls into the central courts and the Master's throne room, but again, through some trick of the tapestries, I followed hall after hall around the building with no greater success than I'd had in finding my own room.

Eventually the castle bell rang again, only from inside, it sounded muffled and seemed to come from far away. Almost immediately, the silent people began to file slowly through the halls talking quietly to each other. My old acquaintance appeared with the others, and when he noticed that I was making my way in his direction, he smiled and waved cheerfully. He took my arm and walked with me along the seemingly endless halls, chatting in the same subdued tone of voice that everybody else used.

"I am so glad to see you again," he said. "It has been a long time since we last met, hasn't it?"

"Much too long," I agreed quietly, following his example by keeping my voice down to just above a whisper. Deciding to come right to the point, I quickly asked, "What's going on? Everything is changed since this morning, so much so that I can not even find my own room."

He gave me a look of surprise and then hesitantly answered, "No, nothing's different today."

"But what about the hangings and your silence in the courtyard?" I reminded him, astonished that he would even try to deny the dramatic alterations.

"They are beautiful, aren't they? We greatly honour our beloved Master with our art and our actions."

"Speaking of the Master," I went on, deciding to ignore his refusal to answer my other questions. "I was trying to find him when the bell rang and everybody came inside." If he wasn't going to explain things, I definitely needed to talk to the Master, who I knew would quickly make everything plain.

"Wonderful!" he exclaimed. "We are going into his presence right now…only—" he hesitated and glanced at my armour, "we must not wear our work clothes into his presence."

"I have nothing else to wear until I find my room," I snapped, frustrated at his evasive answers that responded to my questions without providing any real information and perplexed at still having no solution to the mystery of this new state of things.

"Of course," he replied soothingly, as if I were a child. "I think I understand now. You've just arrived and that explains why I haven't seen you in such a long time. Don't worry, though; you will find things quite a bit different here. But once you understand more fully, you will find that you've found a much better place to serve the Master in."

This comment silenced me for a moment as I continued to follow him through the halls and tried to absorb what he had just said.

"Do you mean to say that this isn't the Master's castle?" I finally asked quietly, afraid of the obvious answer that would explain the strangeness of this place.

"Of course it is the Master's palace, or one of them. Only the most dedicated servants of our Master find their way here, where they can serve him even more fully than they could before. Haven't you found your way to us? I guess it's sort of a case of having the right amount of training and getting to the more enlightened state of mind before this palace can even be seen. You've obviously reached that place, so here you are. I apologize for judging you earlier. I thought you were being disruptive purposely for some reason of your own. Some of us are sometimes, you know. The rules can be difficult to follow, and without a lot of discipline, things tend to break out every now and then."

"I've never heard of this," I said cautiously as my mind tried to reject the evidence my senses told me must be true.

"No," he agreed, "we're not taught about this at the first castle because it's something that happens when we're ready for it. If we were prepared ahead of time, then finding this place would be artificial instead of resulting from real growth and maturity."

He led me further through the bewildering maze of hallways and hangings, and I have to admit that I started to feel a little proud that I had grown so much that I was now able to join this more elite group. He finally stopped at one of the doors that, to my uninitiated eyes, looked indistinguishable from any of the others. It opened to his key and he proudly ushered me inside.

It was tiny, dark, and minimally furnished—a stark contrast to the luxurious halls and even to my own room here that have many comforts that he did not enjoy. He quickly lit a lantern and I could see only a small rough bed with a mattress on it that was not as thick as a handbreadth, a tiny stand with a metal basin on it, and a few hooks along the wall where his clothes, consisting primarily of a series of earth-collared robes, were hung. There was no room for anything else and hardly enough room for me to remove my armour and don the scratchy woollen robe that he handed me.

"We live simply here," he commented as he watched me look critically around the room. "All we really need is the Master's presence. In order to show him that all we need is him, we live with only the barest of necessities. Material things only serve to distract our focus from what is really important."

"But the Master wants us to have all good things," I argued quickly, remembering the plenty I had come from.

"Yes, but does that mean that we should take them? Don't you think it shows more honour to do without for his sake?" he countered.

"I always thought he loved the fact that we enjoyed his gifts."

"We are no longer children here; we have grown past those sorts of childish things," he said firmly, in a tone that discouraged me from arguing any more.

Once he was dressed in an outfit virtually identical to the one I wore, he hurried me out of his room, where we joined the group crowded in the hall outside. They were all rushing in the same direction as if they were afraid of being late for something. Following my friend closely and trying to make sense of the tortuous passageways as we went—without much success—I suddenly found myself in a tall, even more elaborately decorated room. It was richly hung with gold, silver and jewel-toned velvet. At the furthest end of the room there was a small square gold and ivory platform that stood a few feet off the floor. Behind it a brilliant white floor-length curtain hung from the ceiling to continually draw the eye back to that central spot.

The large number of people crammed into the room made it crowded, but since all of us stood perfectly still and silent, there was just enough space for everyone. My friend and I found a place among the others and I waited expectantly for the Master to appear, still wondering what to think about all the pomp and splendour around me. I could hardly wait to see his loving smile and gentle eyes again, even though it had not even been an entire day yet since I had last seen him. Part of me dreaded discovering a change in him to match this different setting, but then I could almost hear his own dear voice reminding me that he could never change. There were so many questions that I wanted to ask him and I was excited to be able to show him that I had grown wise enough to find this "Palace of Service," as my friend told me it was called.

We waited a long time before all the remaining stragglers finally filed in and took their places. I wanted to shout at them to hurry so we could see the Master, for it seemed to me as if he would not come until we were all assembled and in order, even though this had never been the case in the old castle, where he seemed to delight in turning up unexpectedly. Finally, all was ready and I eagerly turned my attention to the front and the glowing white curtain. It was certainly more formal and ceremonious than anything I was used to, but if this was what pleased the Master, then I decided that I would enjoy it too. Deep down, though, I was already longing for the joyful informality of the Hall of Music.

When I thought I could stand to wait no longer without raising a shout of impatience, an elderly man dressed in the same robe as the rest of us solemnly walked onto the platform. The room held its breath for an instant as he turned a face full of sadness towards us.

"The Master will not come today," he said in a quiet voice that, in the silence, carried to every corner of the room. "There were reports of speech in the courtyard this afternoon, lagging in work and levity in the hallways."

I felt my friend shuffle uneasily next to me and I was suddenly ashamed of myself as I remembered speaking to him so incautiously as I arrived—even though how I was to know the rule to follow it was more than I could understand. Was it my fault that the Master would not come today? I hung my head, afraid to look at anyone around me, feeling that I personally had been the cause of their missing the pleasure of seeing his face that day.

"You all know that we are here to serve," the elder continued. "We are here to obey and be perfect in his eyes. The Master will not come if we are not worthy; therefore, we must make ourselves worthy because he is worth the effort. We will return to our rooms now, review our behaviour today, and if we find any fault, we must seek deeply for his forgiveness and for strength to do better tomorrow."

With that the speaker left the platform and the people slowly began to file out. Some were crying, others looked resigned; the worst looked as if they had lost all hope of ever succeeding. I turned to my friend with a question on my lips but he shook his head quickly. His eyes held the same great disappointment that I felt in my heart. Without looking to see if I was still following him, my friend hurried away to his room and I felt as if he would have been happier if I had gotten lost along the way. Fortunately, I was quick enough to keep up and he was forced, out of courtesy, to let me in for the second time.

"Has the Master ever come?" I blurted out as soon as the door was closed.

"Not as long as I've been here, but there are stories about a time when…" his voice trailed off sadly. Then he continued, "I can still remember him, you know. Every day we saw him; it was as if he was our friend. But I guess that's how he treats the newest members of his house. Those of us who have known him longer have greater responsibilities and have to meet certain requirements in order to win his favour."

"But what is the use of that if you can never meet those requirements?"

He lifted his head proudly without answering and watched as I began to put my armour back on.

"You do not need that here," he finally commented. "We are far beyond the need of such protection. There are no enemies nearby and only our greater obedience is required to prepare us for more. There are no battles to fight any longer."

I gave him a quick look as the suspicion that he was trying to keep me away from my armour took root in my mind. It was true that I had seen nobody in armour since my arrival, but I also remembered the Master's command to wear that armour always and I had disobeyed that for too long already. As I buckled on my sword, I suddenly felt as if a great lassitude lifted from my mind.

"I will wear my armour until the Master himself appears and orders me to remove it," I said firmly, convinced all at once of the rightness of my decision. I suddenly realized that there was a great deception at work in spite of the pleasant words and great philosophy of my friend. "If we are here to learn greater obedience, then I will continue to obey his last commands to me."

He looked astonished at my bold, almost defiant, speech and then became frightened. He quickly opened the door, and after a glance up and down the hallway, he turned to me with a pasted-on smile.

"Well, it has been nice to see you again. Welcome to the castle. Good luck. I really must be getting to sleep soon—morning comes early, you know," and before I could utter another word, I found myself in the hall facing his closed door.

My suspicions grew as I heard the lock turn, and I became absolutely sure that something was drastically wrong with the castle. I began my long trek through the endless hallways, hoping to find a way out or a way to the truth. I had no greater success finding the exit than I did earlier, when I was searching for my own room and the throne room. It was as if I was trapped on an endless treadmill that took me around in circle after circle, each different enough to keep me hopeful and similar enough to prevent me from finding the way.

I was not even sure that I was in the same hall as the one that held my friend's room, although I had turned into no other. There were no windows to cue me to direction or even to the time of day. I assumed that it was still night since none of the inhabitants were up and moving. It did seem as if it was the longest night I could remember, and perhaps it was, with nothing but the sameness of my footsteps to mark the passage of time.

At last I reached the end of my resources and sat down where I was, right in the middle of the endless hall, to rest. I fell asleep there, and when I awoke, I found myself in the center of a crowd of astonished people. They seemed harmless enough and only stared curiously as I clambered to my feet in my awkward armour.

"Can anyone show me the way out of here?" I finally asked, forgetting that a word spoken during one of the times of imposed silence meant that once again the Master would not come that night.

Curiosity was replaced by anger as they moved together in my direction, unarmed, but just the same, a menacing mob. I drew my sword, hoping that the sight of it would intimidate the group enough to give me safe passage through them. The precious gift of the Master reflected the soft glow of the candles and seemed to take on a light of its own. Then I noticed something else.

As I slowly backed away from the angry group I was amazed to see that the tapestry and the wall of the hall seemed to dissolve when the shine of my sword came close to them. I tried the experiment again and moved the sword right next to the hanging tapestry beside me. It disappeared before my eyes into what looked like nothing more than a grey mist. The people around backed away from me as they also saw the fading of their beautiful hangings and the sturdy looking walls. I passed the sword right through the wall and then cautiously tried it with my hand. You can imagine how excited I was to find that indeed this great stone castle was made of nothing but the same dense grey mist that I had lost my way in the day before.

I walked straight out through wall after wall and even passed right through the shining white curtain that was to act as a foil for the Master when he came. There was absolutely nothing but a solid looking brick wall behind it, so there would have been no way for him to enter the room even if he had desired to make an appearance on their terms. On and on I went until there was nothing left around me but the glory of a grey dawn and the damp forest after a foggy night. I found a place to sit under a tree to wait for the last shreds of the mist to fade away before I tried to find my way home.

Later, when I told the Master about this strangest of all adventures, he explained that I had escaped from one of the greatest of all the enemy's deceptions: the one in which he lures us into service for himself by deluding us into thinking that we have found a higher or a better truth. I realize now that the truth we have here cannot be improved upon. There is no more to it and there is no less than what we've been taught, and that's a really nice thing to know. I took my own lessons from getting into the predicament in the first place. You can laugh if you want, but I went to that poor old horse of mine and humbly apologized to him. All along, I had the key to escape in my hands, but without that single act of true obedience—returning to my armour—I would have been lost forever. It still amazes me that following such a simple, seemingly unimportant rule was the only thing that saved me from destruction.

TWILA'S EYES WERE RIVETED on Marcus' face as he finished. Her lips were slightly parted and her eyes wide. "I had no idea there could be such things as that," she finally commented with a sigh. "You are lucky that you escaped!"

"Not lucky, dear one," the Master said softly. "He obeyed and escaped. There is always an escape if you look for it."

She nodded silently.

"All our rules are meant to keep us safe," Marie stated in her most pedantic teacher's voice. "I know you younger ones, especially, complain about things you don't think are important. Don't think that I don't hear it—I do! Sometimes these things can seem restrictive, but rules are made to be followed."

"Sometimes experience is the better teacher of that lesson," the Master commented gently as he felt Twila shift slightly, attempting to draw away.

"Catherine was one like that," he continued, putting his hand soothingly on hers to keep her close. "She reminds me of you a little bit, Twila. She was small, dark, and quiet, just like you are, and she had a great lesson to learn about rules. But the greater lesson came as a direct result of breaking them."

The dark head returned to its place on his shoulder. "Tell us about it," she said quickly.

Catherine

The Master began . . .

As you know, the grounds of the castle are extensive, to say the least. In summer, lush green lawns stretch over rolling hills that seem to never end, enclosed only by beautiful wooded areas. Around every bend, tree, and shrub is a new marvel just waiting to be discovered; a silver fountain splashes into a glittering pond full of jewelled fish, a sudden profusion of flowers nestles into a hidden space, a surprise discovery of a bountiful harvest hangs from one of the many scattered fruit trees. Even the creatures are gentle and most are unafraid to meet an outstretched hand offering a tasty treat.

For Catherine, as for many others, the garden quickly became her personal place of retreat. She would disappear into the labyrinth depths any time she had a spare moment. Sometimes she would meet me there and we would have a glorious time exploring together. Those were the best times, because I could show her new places that she had not yet found for herself. Even alone, however, she loved to wander over the familiar paths that were ever changing from one season to the next, thinking about the wonderful gifts she had been given and rejoicing over the profound security of her new home.

But one day as she picked a bouquet of flaming red and yellow flowers to take home, she was startled by the voice of a stranger and everything changed. Always wary, she tensed and prepared to run back to the safety of the castle if there was any sign of danger. I had warned her, just as I warn all of you, about the enemies that would try and deceive you into walking away from our friendship. Cautiously, she looked around, hoping to discover the speaker, but he remained hidden in the bushes.

"Who's there?" she called out nervously.

"Nobody important," the unseen voice answered. "I've seen you before and couldn't wait any longer to finally meet you."

A tall, handsome man slowly stepped out from behind the tangled bushes that had concealed him. It flustered her when she realized that he had probably been watching her the whole time she was busy picking her bouquet. His dark hair hung in heavy curls around his face, giving him a youthful, almost boyish appearance, but he had strong, serious eyes that gazed at her with an expression of entreaty and longing. He wore a rich outfit made of what looked like the finest material, and a small jewelled dagger hung at his side.

"Don't run away," he begged as he slowly approached. "I don't mean any harm. I only wanted to meet you and talk for a while, but if you run away I will regret coming forward forever."

Catherine blushed and smiled. There was such timidity combined with naked admiration in his face that she couldn't help but feel flattered.

"I am Aurelius," he said when he had come to within a few feet. He held his hand out so that she had to step forward to take it.

"I'm Catherine," she returned with a shy smile.

He squeezed her hand gently and then released it quickly as if he were afraid of offending her. Although she had never seen him before, she was convinced that he was not one of the enemy's knights. She was sure that he must belong to me, surmising that he had just been away on some sort of quest or mission so his face was not familiar. His next words contradicted that theory but she didn't consider it at the time.

"I've seen you in the garden many times," he told her quietly after gazing at her face for a few minutes. "Do you have any idea how beautiful you are? You're stunning, and I had to tell you today that I love you more devotedly than anyone in this world has ever loved before."

His voice halted a little over this speech, and in spite of thinking that he sounded a little bit ridiculous,

Catherine blushed very prettily and turned away. For a split second she had wanted to laugh at the silly sentimental declaration that sounded like something straight out of the pages of one of her cheap poetry books. Her heavy, dark hair—and skin that she always thought of as too pale—had never seemed to be that special. She could even remember her mother confiding her disappointment at how homely Catherine was to a few friends one afternoon while they shared a quiet cup of tea. The words still resounded in her head and heart the same way as the day she mistakenly heard them. It was almost impossible for her to believe that the stunningly handsome man standing in front of her could imagine that she was attractive enough to bother even approaching, let alone to make a passionate declaration of love to. In spite of her doubts, his words, accompanied by the expression in his eyes, suddenly seemed desperately sincere, and she was flattered.

The bell summoning them to dinner rang and Catherine, surprised at how late it had become, turned towards the castle with a startled exclamation. When she turned back Aurelius was gone. She spent a few minutes searching for him but gave up when the final summons for dinner rang out and she knew that she could not afford to be later than she already was. It amazed her that the young man had been able to slip into the bushes so silently and so quickly. If she saw him again, she was determined to ask him about it, but first she needed to return to the castle and face the consequences of breaching one of the foremost rules about punctuality. Perhaps Aurelius would be there ahead of her, and although she thought it would have been more considerate of him if he had waited so that they could have walked back together instead of disappearing the way he had, the thought of meeting him again hurried her feet almost as much as the fear of facing my disapproval.

As she expected, everyone had already gathered for dinner, and as Catherine tried to slip into her place at the table without being noticed, I tried to catch her eye. Instead of looking up, she concentrated on her plate and ate as unconcernedly as if nothing were out of the ordinary. I decided that I would say nothing to her just then, partly because I knew how her sensitive nature would cringe under a public rebuke and partly to observe her behaviour further. I had never known her to be late before and thought that it must have been something extraordinary that had caused her to be delayed. I hoped, as I always do with all of you, that she would choose to confide in me before I had to ask any questions.

The meal was almost over before she finally had the courage to start furtively glancing around to see if she could spot Aurelius. At first, she couldn't spot him anywhere, and as she began to search for him a little more intently, I managed to catch her gaze several times. Every time, she quickly averted her eyes, and I knew then that there was something that I needed to know about—probably something that she knew I wouldn't approve of.

I watched her file quietly out of the dining room with the others when the meal was over and noticed that she still seemed to be searching for somebody. That was when I called her back. It broke my heart to watch the way she suddenly stiffened at the sound of my voice and returned with reluctance to where I sat. I found out later that just as I called her name she noticed a group of knights across the hall and was hoping to get close enough to see if Aurelius was amongst them before they broke up for the evening. For the first time since her arrival, the thought crossed her mind that I was too demanding. It was not fair that she should have to endure my censure because she wanted to enjoy the company of her new friend and had stayed out in the garden later than usual. When I gently lifted her chin and looked into her eyes, I could see the shame of that thought and the sulkiness slowly drain out of her face.

"My darling daughter," I said as gently as I could, hoping all the time that she would tell me what her trouble was and trust in the love that I have for her. "You need to know that I love you. I have a love for you that will last forever and I will forgive you for any mistakes as long as you come to me like the trusting child you are. Trust me. I am like the best of fathers and have all the good things in the world to offer you."

She nodded as her eyes filled with tears. She felt completely undeserving of the great love that I had just declared to her, yet she still did not tell me what had happened in the garden that day. I saw a renewed determination to love me spring up in her eyes, and for the rest of the evening she did not think of Aurelius again.

It was several weeks before she encountered the handsome stranger again. By that time he had nearly disappeared from her thoughts. She was relieved in a small way, in spite of her initial disappointment, because in not meeting him again she had avoided any challenge to her renewed resolutions to be perfect in following all the rules. She had almost become reconciled to the idea that she would probably never see him again—at least not until her time as a student was over. That day, as she wandered along the outer edges of the garden, he suddenly emerged from behind a grove of trees and wrapped his arms around her before she could utter a word of protest.

"Darling girl," he whispered ardently as he held her struggling body firmly against his, "I thought I was never going to see you again. I was nearly desperate enough to try storming the castle."

Catherine stopped struggling and rested for an instant in his embrace. It felt good to have his strong arms around her and be unable to get away—protected and captivated at the same time. Then, remembering her resolutions, she once again tried to free herself from his increasingly passionate caresses. After another short struggle he finally released her and gave her a triumphant smile. Flustered, Catherine tried to smooth out her rumpled gown and compose her face, which she could feel was hot and flushed with embarrassment and shyness.

"You don't belong to the castle?" she finally managed to ask when she thought her voice would be steady enough. She was disappointed that her first impression of him had been wrong.

"Oh no," he laughed, with just a touch of mockery in his voice. "There is a world outside of this garden, you know, or have you been here so long that you've forgotten that?"

Catherine was a bit offended at his patronizing tone. Of course she knew there was a whole world out there. Hadn't she just come out of it a few short months ago? Did he think she was completely ignorant? Instead of commenting, she turned to walk back in the direction of the castle. She didn't really feel like continuing the conversation, and besides, she wasn't supposed to talk to any outsiders unless they were approved by the Master until more of her training was complete.

"Wait," he called quickly and caught her arm as he guessed that she was leaving. "Don't go yet. We've only just met again and I was completely ignorant to offend you like that. I'm nothing but a pathetic clod." He dodged in front of her and gazed appealingly into her face. "Forgive me?"

Catherine tried to avoid meeting his eyes and then couldn't resist. She smiled slightly and then laughed out loud at the look of relief that flashed over his face when she nodded.

"Please stay and talk to me," he begged. "I love this garden. That's how I found you, and now I love it even more."

She was satisfied. Her vanity blossomed under his obvious desire to please her and she really did want to stay and learn more about this intriguing man. There was no harm in staying a little bit longer, plus she had hours left before she would be late for dinner again.

"Do you know the Master?" she asked as she allowed him to lead her to a fallen tree that made an excellent place to sit and visit.

"We've met," Aurelius answered evasively, then added, "I have a castle of my own on the other side of the valley. You could almost see it from here if it weren't for all these silly trees."

"I thought you were here because you loved those silly trees," she commented dryly.

"I'm here mostly because I like you," he smiled briefly, "and the trees are silly right now because I want to show you my home and they are obstructing the view."

"So you and the master are neighbours, then," she changed the subject quickly, afraid that he was about to embrace her again and not quite sure that she wanted that just yet.

"I suppose so," he said and then paused for a few minutes, gazing at her with a wistful smile. "I wish you could see it," he finally said with a little sigh. "It isn't as spectacular as your Master's castle, but it is my own and I love it."

"Perhaps sometime you can show it to me," she said as she picked up just a trace of his wistfulness. She thought that it would be nice to see his home. She also realized she was becoming more and more interested in everything about him. "I'm sure it is a lovely place," she commented, with the sudden thought that her first answer was somehow not warm enough to satisfy him or adequately express her feelings.

"Well, why not?" he asked impulsively.

"Why not what?"

"Why not come with me now and I'll show it to you?"

Catherine shook her head quickly. It was absolutely forbidden for any of the students to leave the safety of the garden. She prepared herself for an argument and quickly ran through all the reasons why she should insist that she could not go with him. "I can't. If I didn't get back in time for dinner, I would certainly be missed, and we are not to leave the protection of the grounds," she began firmly.

To her surprise he didn't argue, "You're right. Why don't we just walk around for a while instead?"

She was pleased. He hadn't asked her to go against the rules, and his quick agreement that she shouldn't come to see his castle convinced her that he understood her position as a student in the Master's castle. She still felt terribly torn between her feelings of loyalty to the Master and her new desire to know and love Aurelius, but she began to hope that there could be a reconciliation of those two things so she could follow both of the paths in her heart.

They roamed through the denser parts of the garden at a leisurely pace. Aurelius showered her with compliments and gave her every reason to believe that he thought she was the most beautiful woman in the world. Catherine responded to his banter and, to her surprise, discovered herself to be charming. After a while they approached a place where a small clearing revealed the high stone wall that enclosed the garden; she was amazed that they had come so far in what seemed like such a short time. The wall was rough and falling down a little bit in that place and she could see where the moss on the stones was scuffed off. She suspected that this was where Aurelius entered the garden and could see how easy it would be for an agile young man to climb the uneven stonework and leap over to the ground on the other side.

"Would you like to see my horse?" he asked as they came closer to the place. "He's just on the other side of the wall and I can assure you that he is definitely worth seeing. I had him imported five years ago and have never seen his equal before or since."

Catherine hesitated. She knew that the Master had very strictly stated that none of the students should ever venture outside the grounds unattended until they were more prepared for the nature of the warfare they might encounter. It was dangerous and if something happened she would be vulnerable, but then again, she had Aurelius with her. If anything happened, he could be her defender. After all, she knew from the conversation that they had already shared that he was an accomplished warrior, even if he was modestly evasive about his exploits.

"It isn't far," he said persuasively, sensing her hesitation. "I promise you that we will return as soon as you've had a look at him."

As he talked, Aurelius continued to lead the way towards the broken place in the wall and she followed close behind him, struggling with her thoughts.

"I don't know," she said slowly. "I would love to see your horse, but…"

Aurelius turned towards her and kissed her softly. Looking intently into her eyes for a moment, he asked her, "Don't you trust me yet?"

Catherine flushed and turned away for a second. "I trust you," she finally murmured as her feelings began to settle down again. How could she not trust him? If he had meant to hurt her, he had already had ample opportunity. He expressed such warmth and love in everything he did—she suddenly felt sure that he would never do anything to harm her.

Aurelius carefully helped her climb up the stones of the wall and then tenderly lifted her down to the other side. Catherine's heart pounded heavily with a confused mixture of excitement and fear. She was finally truly alone with the one who had won her heart and the excitement of having an adventure outside the confines of the school, even if it was only taking a walk to look at a horse, thrilled her. She refused to think of what the consequences might be if she were caught or if something happened to make her late again. As long as they were not discovered, she was sure that she would be able to slip back over the wall and be demurely sitting at the table when it was time for dinner. Nobody would ever find out, and she promised herself that after this one time she would never break any of the rules again.

Aurelius led the way to a small clearing just out of sight of the garden wall, where his hobbled horse waited patiently. He was truly a magnificent animal with a glossy black coat that shone in the sun, a mane that looked as fine as silk, and an elaborate scarlet saddle with gold trim. Catherine exclaimed delightedly that she had never seen anything so lovely and was thrilled when the horse gently nuzzled her hand with his velvety nose, hoping to get a treat.

"I'll show you how well he goes," Aurelius said enthusiastically, and before she could protest, he set the animal free from its hobbles and leapt lightly into the saddle.

The horse reared slightly at the abrupt addition of his master's weight, but Aurelius was a skillful equestrian and hardly seemed to notice. She was soon laughing and clapping her hands in appreciation as the horse seemed to alternately float around the field and then dance before her eyes.

Then with a suddenness that took her breath away, Aurelius galloped towards her and swept her up onto the saddle in front of him.

"No!" she cried out in fright. "I have to go back!"

"Just a little ride," he said soothingly into her ear. "I'll have you back in no time at all."

She tried to relax and enjoy the feeling of the wind rushing past her face and whipping her hair around, but she became increasingly anxious that once again she would miss the dinner hour, and she was sure that a second infraction would not be treated as lightly and lovingly as the first. Every time she tried to speak, the wind seemed to pull the words away and they flew out of her mouth without drawing even the slightest response from Aurelius. She tried to turn and speak directly to him, but he held her tighter and spurred the flying horse on to even greater speed. She began to struggle, but he squeezed her until she could hardly breathe and had to hold still to keep from fainting.

Finally he shouted into her ear, "Stop it or I'll throw you off and you'll break your idiotic neck."

Frightened at the thought of being flung off the galloping horse and shocked at the sudden cruelty in his voice, she stopped struggling completely and hoped that he would keep his promise and return her to the garden in his own time without any more arguing from her. They had been gone long enough that she was sure she would be late and her little escapade would not remain undiscovered. She held on to the thought that he was only playing some sort of lover's joke on her and that soon they would get back. At the worst, if she annoyed him any more, she thought he might set her down somewhere in the wilderness that flew past them and leave her to walk back on her own.

At first it did not even occur to her that he had any intentions other than to take her for a ride and show off his horse, but when they did not turn back towards the garden she realized, with a flood of panic, that she had put herself entirely in his power. Even then, she could not imagine that he would ever do anything to harm her; he had so totally convinced her that he loved her—she just wasn't sure anymore that he cared about the rules of the castle or the consequences to her for breaking them.

The speed still kept her from trying to plead with him to take her back quickly, and after his ugly threat to throw her off the horse, Aurelius was also silent. They rode until long after the sun had set and Catherine's body ached with fatigue as every stride sent a little jolt of pain shooting through her. Finally they crested a high hill and she looked down into a dark valley that in the twilight seemed to have no bottom to it at all. The dim outline of an enormous castle that was situated against a high cliff at the most distant end was just visible in the dim light. She suddenly realized that this was their destination as he wordlessly turned the horse's head down a steep trail. She wondered how they would find their way in the dark, but the horse was surefooted and seemed to be familiar with the path. Aurelius never hesitated at all, and in spite of her fear, she felt a renewed confidence in him.

She remained still and silent, fuming over the trick he had used to bring her there. As soon as she had her feet safely on solid ground she was going to tell him exactly what she thought of him, and then, somehow, she would find her way back home as quickly as possible. She was determined, no matter if he said he loved her or not, she was not going to spend a single night under the same roof as him. There was nothing but anger and disappointment in her heart, and more than anything else, she never wanted to see him again. If only it could have been that easy to take back the decision that took her over the wall with him in the first place!

Even though it was clearly visible, it took a long time to reach the castle. When they finally arrived, it was dark enough to require the dim reddish light that showed the way across a short drawbridge that ended at an enormous black gate. It was cold in the deep shadows of the valley and she shivered as the horse's hooves rang hollowly over the wood. She could hear the gentle rippling sound of slow moving water and realized that there must be a moat. The gate and drawbridge were probably the only entrance to the forbidding castle. Her heart sank as they clattered through the yawning black opening into a wide courtyard and Aurelius growled out an order to raise the drawbridge. He continued to hold her in his iron grip until the grinding mechanics of the heavy bridge had completed their work and the iron gate slammed shut with a metallic bang. Only then did he push her unceremoniously off the horse so that she landed on the ground in a heap of aching bones.

"Take her to the tower," he ordered as he dismounted and handed the reins of the horse to a nearby servant.

In the dim light she could not see his face, but it seemed to her that his voice had changed from the soft gentle tones of love to something harsh and brittle. It impressed her with a sense of calculated cruelty, and for the first time she fully understood that he had no good intentions towards her at all. Two armed guards raised her roughly to her feet. As soon as he saw that she could not escape, he turned and walked away without looking back.

"Aurelius please listen to me," she called after his retreating form. She would at the very least plead for freedom before she lost what might be her last chance, but his shadowy figure simply melted away into the darkness.

She took a breath to call out to him again, but one of her guards gave her arm a painful squeeze and hissed in her ear, "Shut up." For a moment the pain made her breathless. She was sure that he would break the bone if she so much as whispered a complaint. They led her toward the opposite part of the castle from where Aurelius had gone, to a large dark door at the bottom of one of the turrets. As they approached, it swung open like a dark mouth ready to swallow them.

Where the courtyard had been dark, the blackness inside the tower was so thick as to be an almost palpable heaviness that felt as if it would choke her. Instead of taking a torch to light the way, the guards, either very familiar with the tower and its stairs or able to see in the dark better than she could, pulled her roughly up a steep flight of stairs that were uneven enough to cause her to stumble at every step. They went along, yanking her up bodily by the arms every time she fell, bruising and scraping her shins against the rough stone. As her eyes grew more accustomed to the darkness, she could make out the dim doorways that they passed and she wondered how many other prisoners were housed there. The building was silent except for their footsteps, but that did not mean that she was the only one. Finally, after climbing to what she imagined must be near the top of the tower, they stopped outside one of the doors and pushed it open. With a rough shove they pushed her inside, laughing as she stumbled over the threshold and fell in a sprawled heap on the floor. Then the door slammed shut and she was alone.

The rock floor was as cold as ice, but she continued to lay there for a time, trying to gather her numb senses into some sort of order. The sound of screaming suddenly shattered the stillness. In the dark, Catherine curled up and let her tears stream unheeded from her closed eyes. This, then, was the end. She had allowed herself to fall into evil hands and she knew Aurelius was not going to let her go.

The screaming continued until she thought she would go crazy, and then, just as suddenly as it had started, it stopped, leaving a silence that killed the last bit of hope in her heart.

At first she expected all sorts of horrible things to happen. She lived her days on edge, listening for the sounds of footsteps ascending the stairs to her prison and dreading the moment when the closed door would swing open, only to quiver with relief when it was only the keeper bringing her food or a jug of water. A small opening cut between the top of the wall and the edge of the roof let in the only light. She spent time watching the small sliver of light crawl across the wall opposite the window, measuring the hours of the morning by the distance between bricks. She very quickly lost track of the days and submerged into oblivion while she crouched dully on the small bench that was the only piece of furniture in the room. Human time was marked only by the regular visits of the keeper.

Aurelius made a single appearance to gloat over his conquest, and even then he seemed slightly bored with the whole thing. He came one day in the early weeks and gazed at her contemptuously for a few minutes. Then he laughed at her silly attempts to smooth her already matted hair and scrub a little of the dirt from her unwashed face with hands that only made matters worse.

"Did you really think that I was in love with you?" he said derisively. "You? Look at you! You may not have been much before, but now you are less than nothing. You knew then that you were a worthless nobody, but you drank up every word I said as if you thought you might be a princess after all!"

His laughter echoed through her room, down the stairs, and through her mind so that she knew that she would never forget her shame. He shattered her, disgraced her, and left her alone in the tower from then on to contemplate her foolishness.

Catherine longed to return to her old life but could not imagine ever being able to go back after she had gone willfully in the first place. She believed that even if she could escape she would be rejected. After all, she was the one who had chosen to disobey. I had lovingly warned her and done everything that I could—short of confining her—to keep her safe. How could she ever expect me to welcome her back? How could she even hope that I might? The only hope she had left was for death, but she did not have the will to not eat the poor food they brought to her and no other means of hastening her demise offered a better solution.

One day, as she paced back and forth in the tiny space, she tripped. As she reached out for something to stop her fall, her hand accidentally caught the fine gold chain that hung around her neck and it broke, sending the small pendant that I had given her tinkling to the floor. With a cry of distress, she groped around in the dim light until she found it and pressed it safely in her hand. It was the only thing she had to remind her of her time with us here. She had not given the small pendant with its coat of arms a thought as long as it lay in its place warm against her heart. Like with every other arrival, I had presented the emblem to her on the first day, making my little speech to her about how now she would belong to this household forever and that she should look at it as a symbol of my love for her. It was meant to remind her—and all of you—of all she had come away from on her journey to find me.

As she held it, she noticed that it seemed to begin to glow with warmth of its own. Looking down at the little coin in surprise, she saw that the coat of arms stood out as if it were lighted from within, and for the first time since her capture, she once again felt satisfied and loved. In an instant, her doubts about being accepted again seemed silly as she realized that, no matter what, I still thought of her as my own. After all, I had said on the first day that my love would never change. Of course I still loved her! The revelation of that thought brought on a fresh bout of tears, but they were now tears of joy and hope. She began to feel almost as if I was there with her.

"Open the door and walk out."

The voice startled her. She thought it sounded like my voice, but even in the dimly lighted cell she could see that nobody was really there. No matter how close she felt I was, she still knew that she was alone. She shook her head and laughed a little at her overactive imagination. She even scolded herself for letting the feeling of being close to me play a trick on her mind.

"Try opening the door."

She glanced down at the medallion that still glowed brightly in her hand and, with a sudden surge of assurance, got up and walked over to the door. Her heart thudded painfully as she reached for the handle. She wasn't sure how she would feel if, after all the wonder of that moment, the door was locked. Even though she was alone, she didn't want to feel that she had been silly enough to try the door. Then again, if she didn't try it . . .

It certainly couldn't hurt anything to try the latch, so, trembling with hope, she reached out for the door. To her amazement, the heavy latch lifted easily and the door silently swung inward. She gazed at it in stunned wonder for an instant, then shuddered with the gut-wrenching realization that there was no lock on the door at all. She had naturally assumed that she was locked in her prison and that even making the attempt to open the door would be nothing but a stupid exercise in futility.

She could almost hear the mocking laughter of Aurelius telling his friends about the fool of a girl imprisoned in his unlocked tower room. Even in this he had deceived her.

Clutching her medallion tightly in her hand and allowing the miraculous warmth of it to give her courage, she slowly began to grope her way down the dark stairs. Every minute, she expected to meet the keeper on his way up. If she did, there would be no escape. At every step, she trembled for fear of making a noise that would attract somebody's attention. Every second, she expected to hear the shout that would raise the alarm. Finally, she was at the bottom of the stairs, facing the door that led out of the tower, which was standing slightly ajar. It appeared that the tower was completely unlocked and unguarded. She wondered how long it had been left like that and how long she had unnecessarily remained a prisoner.

Cautiously, she glanced out at what appeared to be a completely empty courtyard. Several hundred feet away she could see the castle gate standing open with the drawbridge down and wondered if she was going to be able to cross the space unobserved. A sense of urgency suddenly possessed her as she realized that the time the keeper usually appeared with food was fast approaching. She had to make the attempt or lose her chance altogether.

With her heart thudding, she slipped into the shadow of the tower and tried to walk like she knew where she was going and had business to attend to. Staying in the shadows of the building, she hoped if anybody did see her they would not take any notice. The closer she got to her goal without any sort of alarm being raised, the more she had to fight the temptation to run madly towards the open gate, knowing that if she suddenly bolted she would be more likely to attract attention. The gate loomed closer and closer until, with her heart nearly choking her, she was about to step out past the walls of the castle and onto the dark wooden bridge.

A cold laugh stopped her in her tracks. Aurelius stepped out of the shadows on the opposite side of the drawbridge and took a few steps towards her so that her way was blocked. He leered at her with an evil grin and then laughed so that his mockery seemed to ring all the way down the valley.

"It took you long enough to find your door unlocked! Where do you think you're off to now that you're onto that little trick of mine?"

"I am returning to my Master."

"Do you think he wants you?" he asked contemptuously. "Just look at you: you're dirty, smelly, skinny, and uglier than ever. There are a lot of better people out there, so what makes you think he wants you back after you lied to him and disobeyed his rules? Sorry sweetie, but you're damaged goods now. He'll never forgive you for that. You'll never be of any value again and he'll just throw you out the minute you get there."

For an instant she wavered. After all, weren't these the very same thoughts and doubts that tormented her when she thought of going back? Aurelius was quick to see his advantage and took a step closer to her.

"You could stay here and serve me," he offered softly. "Not in the tower, of course; I'll give you proper rooms and teach you, just like he would have. I know this wouldn't have been your first choice, but isn't any home better than no home at all? All you need to do is throw that little trinket of yours into the moat and I'll take care of everything else."

She was reminded of the pendant that was still clutched in her hand, instilling a sense a warmth and peace into her heart in spite of the menace of Aurelius. A sudden fear gripped her as she thought that he might have the power to take it away by force, and she clutched it fiercely to her chest. The metal once again seemed to develop a heat of its own and she felt a wave of calm flow over her.

"I belong to the Master of the Music," she said boldly. "You cannot touch me. Now let me pass!"

With a cry of rage, Aurelius grew larger and blacker until he towered over her in the shape of a gigantic black dragon. With eyes that glowed red with fierce hatred, he snarled angrily and made a feint in her direction, as if he would knock her off the drawbridge into the water below. Catherine, filled with an inexplicable sense of calm courage, walked steadily towards the monster. With each step, he retreated the same distance that she moved, snarling the whole way until she forced him off the bridge completely. With a final cry of rage, he flew at her again, trying to force her to give ground and retreat back onto the bridge.

She shook her head and walked away from him and his horrible castle. She could hear him roaring furiously in the darkness behind her and wondered at the strange boldness that had just set her free from him. The sounds behind her were dreadful and made her shudder, even now that she was safely out of his reach and having just proven that he could do nothing to her. Her path lay before her, glowing in the moonlight. The horror that she left behind could never touch her or be a part of her again—she was going home.

At the top of the valley, she met the troop of horsemen that I had sent out to find her. They had been searching for her for many days and were almost on the point of turning back when she appeared with the sunrise at the top of the enemy's valley. It was a wonderful day when she came back, and I was so proud of all that she had learned on the journey—not that I recommend that kind of learning.

"I LIKE THAT," Twila said quietly. "She shouldn't have done what she did, but because of it she found out even more about how much you love her."

Marcus agreed quickly, "All the training in the world couldn't have prepared her for the future as much as that one battle with Aurelius. The key is to learn about the extent of the power of the Master's love."

"But was it your voice that she heard in the tower, Master?" Twila asked.

The Master smiled mysteriously and didn't say anything.

Timothy shifted in his chair and coughed nervously. The Master looked in his direction and smiled. "Remind you of anything, Timothy?"

"Well, it made me think a little bit about how I didn't have to wander off to find myself in a bit of a fix," he commented softly. "My problem came more out of not wanting to wander off."

"Do you want to tell us your story?" asked the Master.

Timothy

The quiet, grey-haired man with striking blue eyes shuffled uneasily in his chair for a moment before he very shyly began to speak in a low voice. Marie quickly complained that she couldn't hear him. With a soft apology and a visible effort to speak louder, he began his story again.

I CAME TO THE MASTER as an older man and, like the rest of you, he took me in with open arms. Very soon I found my place in the garden, tending to the plants and helping them grow. I spent years there, just loving things and helping them become the most beautiful or fruitful that they could be. Don't think that it was an easy job, either. There were always pests to control, weeds to pull, pruning, staking, dividing, trimming, and of course, watering. It was amazing to me how moving a single plant from one bed to another could reinvent both places in totally new ways. The new bed could be livened up by the addition of a different flower or foliage and the old would suddenly come forward with plants that perhaps had been too crowded or overshadowed before but were given a new chance to shine out. But then, you did not all come here for a lesson on gardening.

One day the Master summoned me to the throne room, which surprised me, since most of the time he came to me in the garden and we enjoyed our time gloating over the new and the old together and perhaps making plans for changes as we walked. When I arrived, the Master smiled at me so kindly that I thought I would die of his love right there. I just knelt at his feet and waited for him to begin.

"Timothy," he said, speaking gently and raising me to my feet, "I have a quest for you. It's a new task and a new place for you to go."

I was shocked into silence. The first thing that popped into my head was that somehow I had failed in my work in the garden and that he was sending me away in disgrace. I was so ashamed that I couldn't even raise my head to look at him, let alone speak. Perhaps he saw my tears; I don't know.

"You have been faithful in your place," he said reassuringly after a few minutes, as if he had read the very thoughts that were in my mind. "I know you can do what I have for you and there are others who will fill the place you leave behind."

I still could not speak, and a few minutes later I felt his hand press my shoulder as he left the room.

He did not even tell me then what my new task would be!

I remember how I staggered to my feet and stumbled all the way back to my room. As my shock began to subside, I suddenly found myself deeply and bitterly angry with my beloved Master. He had given me no reasons for the change. He had just announced it and left me no choice or recourse. He had not even asked if I were willing. The bitterness of my heart rose into my throat like gall, and as I stayed awake thinking about it, I choked on the same thing over and over again.

The next morning I went out to the garden just like usual. I decided to work in the most remote corners of the grounds, hoping that as long as I was out of his sight I would be out of his mind as well and that, in time, he would entirely forget about the change he had spoken of. I remained angry, and everything I put my hand to that day only seemed designed to make me even angrier than I already was. I discovered aphids that had been overlooked by one of the under-gardeners and that had nearly destroyed a rare rose bush. Weeds had sprung up overnight. Clipping turned into an exercise in frustration as one side or the other kept coming out uneven. Every weed that I touched came off at the ground, leaving the root behind to be dug out by hand. Even the watering pails had developed holes overnight, it seemed, and I needed to make twice as many trips to the well as usual. At the end of the day I was hot, tired, and entirely frustrated with the garden in general and the Master in particular.

Later in the evening, he came to the garden and called me, but I pretended I didn't hear him and walked in a direction that I knew would take me farther from his voice instead of nearer. He did not call again, but I knew that if he had assumed that I had really not heard his call he would wait for me near the gate, so I went the long way through the garden and entered the castle through the back entrance that night.

Day after day it was the same. I began to feel as if nothing that my hands touched would ever grow or prosper. I became morose and silent. No one could talk to me without getting growled at for the effort. Soon I was left entirely alone except for every afternoon when the Master would walk through the garden and call to me. Sometimes I heard him and sometimes I didn't, but I knew that he always came. Sometimes I planned for his arrival and would go to the furthest corners of the grounds so that I could not hear him. It almost became a sort of game I played, to see how many days I could escape the sound of his voice before I would find that I was close enough to hear it again.

I suppose things could have gone on that way for a long time, but one day when I arrived there was a young, energetic, pathetically eager boy waiting for me by the tool shed. I think I growled some sort of greeting at him—you know, the sort that should have made him hightail it back to wherever he had come from. At any rate, it didn't work. Instead, he told me that the Master had sent him to learn about the gardens from me. Instead of listening to all of my grunts and growls of discouragement, he followed me everywhere I went that day, watching what I did and asking the occasional question, which I mostly ignored. Of course, I realized that this young man was meant to be my replacement, and I was determined that nothing I did would help him take my place. However, he not only had a green thumb, but he must have had green fingers and green toes as well, because the garden began to flourish again under his care. When I saw that, I quit going to the garden at all.

I think I spent another week sulking in my rooms, and it was one of the longest weeks of my life. All that I had been to the Master was gone. I had been rejected, made supernumerary. I had no friends left. I had no place or purpose. I did not even really have the Master anymore since I had been so diligent to avoid him and hadn't spent any time with him in months. All I had left was my anger and the bitter root that had now grown firmly into my heart. At the end of that week I decided that it was time to leave. I packed a few belongings and headed for the gates. And wouldn't you know it? There was the Master, waiting for me just as if he had nothing else in the world to do. He gazed at me with eyes filled with love and not even a hint of reproach, even though he knew I had been avoiding him. I felt as if my heart was being torn out of my chest as I suddenly realized all that I was about to walk away from.

I will never be sure how it happened, but I found myself sobbing in his arms and heard his gentle voice soothing and comforting me. Then he asked, "Are you ready now to go where I ask you to go and do what I need you to do?"

There was no other answer to give but a strangled "yes." All that had made me refuse to obey him before was gone, and in spite of the rebellion that still wanted to rise up in my heart for a split second, I knew that the alternative was no alternative at all. I felt as if my whole life had been emptied out, and even so, I had been about to trade the only thing that meant everything for nothing at all.

Then he told me about his new plan for me and sent me on my first quest for a certain rare and exotic plant that he wanted to obtain for the garden. He said that he wanted me especially for the job because he knew that I had the ability to nurse the plant on the journey home so that it would be healthy and strong when it arrived here. The thought of the journey frightened me—and it was difficult, even dangerous sometimes—but what a joy to finally discover the plant I had been searching for, coddle it all the way home, and then see it flourish in the garden under the skillful hands of that boy who took over my old job.

"We often resist at first, don't we?" Marie commented thoughtfully when Timothy was finished talking. Without thinking, she touched the three parallel scars on her cheek. "Then all of a sudden we end up in the most unexpected places, only to discover that the unexpected place is the very place we belong in after all."

The Master shifted slightly and put his arm around the teacher.

"It took a while for you, but you finally got there, didn't you?" he said tenderly.

"Yes," she said quietly. "I got there."

Marie

I GREW UP IN THIS CASTLE. My parents came here as young people a long time before I was born, and I knew no other life. I suppose I should have been grateful, and in many ways I was, especially when I saw some of the miserable creatures that dragged themselves over the threshold to fall breathless and exhausted into the Master's waiting arms. I wondered sometimes how he could do it when the stench of their filth filled me with revulsion—and I wasn't the one standing close enough to touch them. I was grateful that the circumstances of my birth had saved me from the kind of life that brought them to such a desperate state. I did not think I could survive the horrific experiences some of them later described. People truly do hideous things to themselves and to each other, don't they?

I guess it started when I began to think about the joyfulness I was seeing in those who found new hope in the palace. They had a freedom and an exuberance that I could not relate to. I had all of the same things they now did, but I was so used to them that they were no longer exciting for me, I suppose. They belonged to the Master and were beloved by him as I remembered being with my mother and father as a very young child. I knew and loved him as a matter of course, but I slowly developed a tendency to look on and smile aloofly at the antics of the newcomers, feeling a strange mixture of superiority and longing to join in.

It would have wounded me deeply if anyone had ever accused me of taking everything that I had for granted, but in fact, as I look back, that was exactly what I did. I assumed that because he had always been there, he always would be. I felt that I was somehow protected from the evils of the world around me by virtue of my birth and residence in the palace. I handled the treasures of the kingdom with the carelessness of familiarity, never suspecting for a moment that everything could change.

When I was just eighteen, I went out on a training exercise in the forest with a group of students all about the same age as me. I spent the afternoon lounging idly, watching the others practice swordplay and self-defence for what seemed like the millionth time in my life. There were a few newer members of the class that could not seem to catch on to even the most basic techniques. At first I tried to help one of the girls near me who seemed to me to be in imminent danger of putting the sword through her foot—or mine—but everything I told her seemed to confuse her more. I ended up telling her to wait for the teacher who was better at explaining things and then left the field in disgust.

A short distance away, I found a quiet place where I could sit and watch without being particularly obvious and waited for lunchtime to come. At the time I knew it would have been better to stay and help out, but I told myself that I didn't have the patience for teaching and that I would probably be more helpful where I was. I'm not sure how long I sat daydreaming before a ripple of excitement passed through the rest of my class and I saw the Master standing among them.

"He would show up on the day I'm sitting on the sidelines," I thought, a little bitterly.

It had been a long time since the Master had dropped in on my class and even longer since he had given me any personal acknowledgement. I wanted him to notice me and approve of me but he never did. It frustrated me that he had arrived on the day that if he noticed me at all it would be with disapproval for shirking practice.

I could almost hear his quiet, steady, uncompromising voice saying, "Marie, you know we are all like one body—working together, supporting one another, and holding on to each other. If one part of your body isn't doing its part, your whole body suffers, doesn't it? It is the same with us."

I sighed, disgusted with myself, and tried to become very small and still where I sat. Perhaps he would overlook me sitting there so quietly and I would escape his lecture, if there was going to be one.

He slowly made his way through the group of my classmates. Each one eagerly awaited his touch and words of instruction or encouragement. The girl I had tried to help trembled a little as he approached. She still had not had time with the teacher, and out of all of us, she was doing the worst. From where I sat, I could see the Master's gentle smile as he kissed her cheek and then quietly showed her how to hold her sword, thrust, parry, and counter. As the lesson went on I caught a glimpse of her face. It simply shone with wonder that the great Master was beside her, helping her and laughing with her as she learned.

Suddenly tears sprang to my eyes as I realized that this was what I longed for from him but I was already skilled at using the sword. I did well in all my studies and I could think of nothing that I needed help with.

As I continued to watch the lesson, he suddenly looked up and straight into my eyes as if he could read my jealous thoughts. He said nothing, but I caught a glimpse of his disappointment in me before he turned his attention back to the girl he was working with. I was as miserable as I had ever been in my life, and as soon as I was sure that nobody would notice, I slunk quietly away to hide my shame in the woods.

After a while the feeling of embarrassment and shame turned to anger. He had not even thought enough about me to come and tell me that I had done wrong. It had been months since he had even noticed that I existed, and then the first time I sat out a lesson he showed up to condemn me and share his presence with everybody else.

Even as I argued for my anger, I knew that I was being unreasonable. If I had chosen then to go to him and talk to him about it, he would have sat down with me with the same love and kindness that he always showed me; it was my own actions that had caused me to miss out on his visit. My own coolness tempered his response to me, and he didn't have to take the time to come over to tell me that I had done wrong when I already knew for myself that I should have been with the group. After all, who was I to expect him to come and spend time with me when there were so many others that needed him more than I did?

As I walked, I came to a grassy little hollow a short distance away from the meadow with a tiny stream running through it. I was close enough to hear the noise of the class and the walls of the castle were nearby for safety. After the first fury of my anger was over, I rested and listened to the burbling of the brook, the rustle of the leaves in the gentle fingers of the wind, the buzzing of various insects busily going about their work, and the cheerful chirping songs of the birds. The peaceful forest that surrounded my home wrapped me in its arms and lulled me to sleep.

When I awoke it was cold and dark. The forest was deathly still so that the only thing I could hear at first was the sound of my own breath coming and going. Even the sounds of the brook were strangely muffled, and an icy finger of fear sent a chill up my spine. I felt as if I were being watched, so I lay still, pretending that I was asleep as I tried to remember which direction I needed to run in order to reach the gates of the castle.

Stealthily I felt for my sword, which was normally strapped to my waist, but with a shock of remembrance I realized that I had left it behind at the edge of the meadow. I'm not sure that even then I fully realized the acute danger I was in. At first I thought that, as long as I remained still, there was a chance I could escape unnoticed and whatever was there would pass me by. I even thought for a moment that, as a member of the Master's house, I could not be harmed, forgetting that I had left its protection and come away on my own. I understood later that I was protected even then to a certain degree, but the choices I made that day made me more vulnerable than I knew.

With a sudden unearthly shriek, a bat-like shape plummeted out of the dark branches that obscured the night sky at the edge of the clearing. I saw it coming just in time to escape being crushed to death in its claws, but with a vicious swipe it left three bloody gashes across my cheek before it flew into the air again. As if this initial attack were a signal, I was immediately surrounded by a group of howling, moaning, hissing creatures that had been hidden in the trees all around me. I cowered helplessly in the hollow, as I could see no way of escape, and waited for the expected rending and tearing to begin. After a few seconds, I remembered some of the things I had been taught so many times and decided that, despite missing my sword, I needed to do my best to resist the attack. Even if I could only destroy a single one of the hideous things before I was killed, there would at least be one less of them in the world to torment someone else.

    I gathered my strength, and with what I hoped was a courageous sounding cry, I took the offensive and rushed straight forward in the direction that I thought might lead me back to the castle. If there was any possibility of breaking through, I wanted to be as close to rescue as possible. As I reached the first clump of bushes, I was swarmed by a shrieking mass of pinching, biting, scratching, snarling creatures that I could not have imagined in even the worst of nightmares. The sheer weight of them pushed me to the ground where, one by one, I grasped them and threw them off. Another immediately replaced each one that I pulled away so that I was never really any further ahead in spite of all my efforts. Very slowly, I crawled through the forest. High overhead, the bat creature screamed out its wrath—a sound that brought tears of terror to my eyes every time I heard it. Finally, just as dawn was breaking, I lay down, exhausted by the battle and prepared to die of the nagging little pains that I thought were going to destroy me tiny bit by tiny bit.

Then, with the rising of the sun they were gone. Weakly, I raised my head but there was no joy in my release. I was dirty, tattered and covered with bloody wounds. Every part of my body seethed with pain and I did not even have the energy left to call out for help. I slept for what must have been several hours before I was awakened by hunger and a burning thirst. I managed to find my way to the side of the small stream, where I drank and ate a few berries that grew on some bushes along the banks. Then I slept the sleep of complete exhaustion again.

I awoke again just as night was falling and realized that my only chance of survival was to return to the Master. So making what I thought was a good estimation of where the castle should be, I walked as quickly as I could—which didn't turn out to be very fast at all—in that direction. However, I only got a few steps away from the creek before the swooping form of the bat struck me on the head and knocked me to the ground. With a gasp of pain and terror at the idea of spending another night in torment, I managed to make my way back to the edge of the water, where I curled up in a ball with my back against a tree and waited for the inevitable.

The night remained quiet, but not the muffled unnatural silence of the night before. The chattering water nearby seemed like good company, but even so, the rising sun found me still awake and trembling with the cold. It was damp beside the water and the ground where I cowered was marshy. I felt as if I were chilled right to the bone. As I shivered and tried to stretch out my cramped, aching limbs, something even colder suddenly touched my neck. Almost as soon as I felt the chill of it flood through my body, a serpent was wrapped tightly around me. A small voice hissed some incoherent words into my ear, and with a scream, I grabbed the slimy creature and tried to pull it off. The more I pulled, the tighter it clung and the more often I felt the piercing pain of its teeth as it bit my hands, face, and ears until I let go and the snake once again settled into its original position around my neck. I decided that the only solution would be to get back to the castle as soon as possible and beg the Master to help me.

"Where are we going?" the voice suddenly hissed in my ear as I started walking through the forest at a fairly determined pace.

We were taught to never enter into any discussion with an enemy so I ignored the voice.

"I said, where are we going?" This time the thing accompanied its question with a hiss and a painful bite on my cheek.

I yelped in surprise and then replied quietly and firmly, "Back to the Master."

"Oh, very well then."

I walked on for a while, not at all sure that I was going in the right direction but not wanting to seem uncertain to my uninvited guest.

"Do you think he'll want you back?"

I had not thought of this and the idea stopped me in my tracks. With a quick glance down at my hands and clothes, I realized what a mess I was. If anything, I was worse off than most of the ones that I used to pity as I watched them cross the castle gates for the first time. It was inexcusable that someone like me, who knew better than to make the mistake of wandering off into the forest alone without their sword or armour, should appear at the gate in a more wounded and bedraggled state than someone who could not even recognize the enemies that were out there.

"You should clean up a little bit first, don't you think?" the voice suggested smoothly.

I did not say anything to the snake, but I did agree, and when we came across yet another little stream I bent to wash myself. It was strange, but the more I tried to wash the dirt and blood off, the worse the mess became. Finally, with tears of frustration in my eyes, I left the stream and walked on.

"Maybe there will be a better stream a little further on," the voice hissed in a mocking tone.

I decided to look for one. I was no longer concerned about getting to the castle as quickly as possible. I was suddenly worried instead that I would stumble on it and be unable to hide my filthiness in time. As much as I wanted to be near to the Master again, I could not stand the thought of his disappointment in me or the looks that I expected to see in the eyes of those who were used to looking up to me as an example.

The snake remained fastened around my neck, and any time I tried to pull it away it would bite and choke me until I had to stop and leave it alone. I wandered for days and days. I wanted so much to return to my home and my Master, but I could not bring myself to appear before him in such a terrible condition. Sometimes I saw his knights riding through the forest, seeking people who needed help and fighting battles with the dark ones. But I would hide from them in my shame and cling to the pride that kept me from admitting my condition. A single cry would have broken that pride and summoned the help that I so desperately needed. But I never uttered that cry. My soul longed to return. My hunger to see the face of the Master became even greater than my hunger for food, and I began to linger near the highways, hoping to catch a glimpse of him as he passed by. I watched his servants when they came past, for I could sometimes just catch a reflection of a part of him in their faces. Yet I remained unseen: hidden, fouled, and dirty.

I found endless waters to wash in and all were the same, only creating more dirt and more damage than before. In time even my clothes were hardly enough to cover me and my new shame at my nakedness made my movements even more careful and furtive.

I suppose I would have gone on in the same way until I died—and I nearly did—if it hadn't been for one of those miraculous accidents that sometimes save us. It happened on a day when I was lingering near the highway. I heard the sounds of travelers, and thinking that I would get a better view from the other side of the road, I tried to rush across before they came along—only I had grown so weak and was so clumsy that when I tripped and fell in the middle of the road I was not able to get up fast enough to hide again. As the riders approached, I hid my face and struggled to get off the road before they could see or recognize me.

"They're coming! They're going to see you! You're dirty and naked! You must get off the road!" the hissing voice shrieked in my ear. "You're too horrible to be seen! They'll find out about..." Then it suddenly fell silent.

The riders had stopped and there was silence except for the sound of my sobs and the soft breathing of the horses. Finally, without looking to see who it was, I said, "Please help me."

At the first touch, I knew that it was the Master. A faint hissing shriek, and the tight band around my neck disappeared along with the fear that he would reject me. I remember trying to kiss the foot that I could see next to me but there was no time before I was lifted into his strong gentle arms and I could gaze into his majestic, beautiful face. To my surprise, his face, like my own, was covered with tears of joy. There was not even a hint of reproach, even though I wanted to start on myself for doubting his love in the first place. He wouldn't even allow that.

I knew then the sheer joy of his love and I know it now. I have never learned patience—he gave it to me. I have never learned to love—he gave that to me as well. And of all the places he could have asked me to fill, I am a teacher. It's not because I'm a naturally great teacher, but because I need him most when I try to do the things that are the most difficult for me. With his help, I am better at teaching than I was at anything else that I ever tried.

THEY SAT IN SILENCE for a while. Twila and the other students had often wondered about the scars on the teacher's face, but none of them had managed to find the courage to ask her about them. How often had she complained that Marie seemed impossibly unapproachable and uncompromisingly strict? She knew better now. Like herself, Marie was still learning and growing. Apparently it took a lifetime to learn the music of the Master.

She thought of the wicked creatures that lurked in the forest all around them and shivered a little bit. She was thankful that, so far, all her work had kept her mostly indoors.

"There are many creatures that serve the enemy," Marcus finally commented, "but most of them are not difficult to defeat in battle. It's when your arms are neglected that you're going to get into trouble."

"That's true," the Master agreed. "The servants of the enemy are at a disadvantage when faced with one of us fully armed and prepared for battle, but sometimes more is required. None of you has yet encountered a true fiend, one of the most powerful fighters that the enemy has. That's because nearly all of them were taken prisoner years ago when the first great battles were fought. They haven't been destroyed, though, because sword and steel won't do the work."

"Our very own captain of the guards could tell you how to defeat that kind of evil creature, but since Captain Joshua isn't here, perhaps Marcus knows enough of the tale to tell it—if you would like to hear it, of course, and if he's willing to tell another story."

They all nodded eagerly as Marcus glanced around for their answers. Captain Joshua was almost legendary amongst them for his bravery and cunning. There lingered a mystery about him, however, that most of the inhabitants of the castle could only speculate about. Perhaps this story would shed some light on the special relationship that was so apparent between the Master and his captain. As captain, he would not have had to give way to anyone, but more often than not, he could be found doing little things to help out others and there was nothing that seemed to be too menial for him to do for somebody else.

Joshua

Marcus began with a smile, "It happened a long time ago, shortly after Josh first arrived here as a young student…"

He leaned back on his pillows one night and gazed up at the trapdoor, just as he had done several nights running—actually every night since he had first moved into the room. What could be so important that it would be stored up there? And why was he forbidden to see it? Maybe it was treasure. Somebody had to have money to keep the school and the castle running. Everyone that he had talked to had come to the Master with no money at all; in fact, most of them had arrived needing absolutely everything, even the clothes on their backs. Everything had been provided for them: their tattered, travel-worn clothes were exchanged for white linen garments with the emblem of the Master stitched across the front; their hungry bellies were filled with hearty, nutritious food; and they were given shelter in the rooms of a castle more luxurious than anything any of them could have imagined. It must be treasure, he decided, and he turned over and tried to think about something else.

The Master had been very serious about his not opening the door. Joshua had even been a little frightened at the stern look on his kind face as he gave the warning. He didn't think it would be such a big deal if he saw a bunch of money, or even gold or jewels hidden in the attic. He knew that he had never stolen anything in his life, even when the temptation was there and it would have been so easy. Nobody would have to worry about that. Of course, that was exactly what the Master told him when he showed him his new room: they trusted him especially. Josh smiled proudly. He would never do anything to break that trust.

However, there could be no harm in speculating about what was behind the door, since he was determined to never open it. It didn't have to be a treasure. After all, the old castle was a pretty strange place with who knew how many secrets hidden behind other doors just like this one. Maybe it was something dangerous—but then it couldn't be anything alive. There hadn't been a sound in the attic since he had moved in a week ago. If anything, it must be treasure or some other valuable thing. The most reasonable thing was that the Master wanted simply to make sure that he didn't fall and get injured by trying to climb up and explore the attic. After all, the trap door was very prominent and very enticing, and most boys would be tempted at some point to want to see what was on the other side.

"I've climbed into worse places and fallen from higher ones," he muttered quietly under his breath. "If I was going to climb up there I'd just move the desk over under the door and then put the chair on top of that. I wouldn't have to stretch to reach at all and it would be almost impossible to hurt myself."

Josh got up from the bed and restlessly paced around the room. Why did they make bedtime so early? It was only nine-thirty according to the clock next to his bed and he didn't feel tired at all. Just think of all the fun they could be having if the rules were more relaxed about bedtime. He sat down at his desk for a while and tried to read one of the massive textbooks on true knighthood, but it was useless. He was bored and his mind continually returned to focus on the mystery of the attic above his head. He sighed as he got up from the desk and started pacing around the room again.

"I don't suppose it would do any harm if I just had a quick look. I know I can get up there without falling, and it sure would be a great thing if there really was a treasure hidden up there," he said to himself as he thought of the fun it would be just knowing that kind of secret.

The Master's words on the first day of classes echoed through the boy's head. "You did not choose for yourselves but were chosen to become men and women of integrity, truth, and honour."

He sighed again and lay down on the bed. His honour was at stake, only it was so aggravating to always just be told what to do and what not to do and never be given any good explanations about things. After all, if he only had been told why the attic needed to remain completely closed up, he wouldn't have been left to wonder about it. It would have been a simple matter of obedience then, and he thought it would have been much easier to obey if the reason was clear. The Master had even cut off his question about the door before he had the chance to ask it. It wasn't fair, and he thought that maybe it proved that he wasn't trusted as much as he thought he was. If there was something in the attic above his room, he had a right to know what it was, didn't he?

After a few more minutes of similar reflection, he jumped angrily off the bed. If they were hiding something, he was suddenly determined to find out exactly what it was; and if they weren't, he would show them that he was old enough to take care of his own safety without having to be given silly rules.

No sooner was his mind made up than Josh went to work to put his plan into action. Cautiously, he slid the heavy desk across the room until it was centered underneath the trapdoor. The old legs screeched horribly as he dragged it along, and he stopped every few minutes to listen at the door for anyone who might come past and look in to investigate the racket. It only took a moment for him to place the chair firmly on top of the desk and clamber up to balance precariously on top. With the guilty feeling that he was being watched, he glanced quickly around the room while he listened quietly for any sound of footsteps in the hall outside his door. All remained quiet and, reassured that discovery was unlikely, he gave the door a cautious push. It was stuck. He pushed harder and it still refused to budge. Finally, mustering all his strength and bracing himself firmly against the chair, he shoved the door upwards with all his might. It gave way all at once and he lost his balance, tumbling to the floor in a tangle of arms and legs and chair.

Bruised, and with the wind knocked out of him, he lay on the floor for a few minutes in stunned silence and tried to catch his breath. He listened anxiously, sure that the noise of his tumble and the crash of the chair would bring somebody to find out what was going on, but still the hall outside his door remained silent. Quietly, he got to his feet and replaced the chair on top of the desk, thankful that, after a quick assessment, he hadn't done anything that looked like permanent damage. He'd have to be more careful.

The trapdoor had fallen back almost into its original place except for a small crack along one edge. He suddenly realized that, with the door fitting so tightly, it might take just as much force from the other side to get it back into place. It would be pretty hard to disguise the fact that he had opened it if he couldn't get it closed again. He decided to worry about it later, and having done so much already, decided to finish the adventure and take a good look around the attic. He could worry about the consequences afterwards if the silly thing wouldn't close up again properly.

Once again balanced on the chair, and carrying a light in one hand, he pushed the door open with the other. This time he was able to raise it easily above his head and managed to slide it off to one side, leaving an opening that he thought would be just big enough to hoist his body through. He was tall enough to put his head entirely through the opening if he stood on the tips of his toes.

To his surprise, the light did not seem to penetrate the darkness at all. It was as if it was misty and the darkness in the attic was thicker than the light. It was dark in a palpable, physical form; the darkness of a being, of an existence—and with a sudden lurch of fear he pulled his head down out of the room and tried to pull the trapdoor closed. There was something there that was far beyond his understanding and outside of anything he had experienced before. It was something that chilled his heart and raised all the childish fears of the dark that he had overcome years ago. Only that old fear was nothing but a crystal clear distillation compared to the heavy vaporous oppression that overwhelmed him now.

The door would not budge no matter how frantically he tugged and pulled on it; something held it back and he could not make it move. As he worked, he saw a pair of glowing red eyes slowly materialize out of the blackness above his head. He tried to close his mind against those eyes and focused instead on pulling even harder at the door, his strength growing weaker even as his terror grew. In a final act of desperation, he opened his mouth to scream for help but it was too late. In a sudden rush his mouth was filled with the black, and it stifled him as he fell beneath the weight of it back off his perch and onto the floor again. The creature poured out of the opening until it virtually filled the room while Josh, in terror greater than any he had ever known before, scrambled into the small square space beneath his desk, hoping that somehow this great evil he had released into his room would forget about his existence and retreat back into its attic prison.

He cringed in his hiding place and watched as the creature swirled around the room, beating against the walls like a caged tornado, shrieking with a voice of wordless fury as it went. He felt its hatred of him. Its anger and desire to destroy filled his heart with dark knowledge and he knew that it wanted to kill him. He also slowly began to realize that for some reason it couldn't.

It seemed like an eternity before the darkness discovered that the window was cracked open to let a little bit of fresh air into the room. Slowly it concentrated itself at the window and began to ooze out. Josh watched in relief as the dark presence slowly decreased and took his terror with it. For the moment he did not care that he was responsible for releasing it into the world at large. All he cared about was that he had survived unharmed and the thing appeared to be leaving. He hoped he would never see it or anything like it again.

When the last remnant of black was gone from the room and the small light that fell onto his bed was able to cast its warm yellow glow into every corner of the room again, Josh rushed out of his hiding place under the desk and slammed the window firmly closed with a bang. Whatever the evil thing was, he was absolutely determined that it would not have a chance to get back in and come after him again. With his heart thudding in fear that there might be something else lurking above his head in the darkness of the attic, he quickly climbed up onto the desk and chair combination for the last time and pulled the trapdoor into place. To his surprise and relief, it moved easily and slid firmly into the opening, looking as if it had never been disturbed at all. He shoved the heavy desk back into its place by the window and pulled the blind closed without looking outside just in case he would see glowing eyes peering back at him through the glass.

After he quickly changed into his pyjamas, he was about to leap into bed when he was startled by a soft knock at the door. With his heart thudding in fear of discovery and feeling guilty at the same time, he asked softly who was there.

The Master's voice came through the door, "It's me. Won't you open the door?"

Josh took a deep breath and walked toward the door. It was one of the Master's habits to occasionally drop in unexpectedly on his students. They were little visits of encouragement or loving instruction that both student and teacher enjoyed. Meetings with the Master were always precious, but having him all to yourself in your own room was stupendous. For the first time, though, Josh's heart did not leap in joyful welcome at the sound of his voice. Instead, he was filled with fear that the Master already knew what he had done. He gave a quick glance around the room and was satisfied that nothing was out of place. He told himself that the Master was there on one of his usual surprise visits and it was just a coincidence that he had come on that night of all nights. Now that the creature was gone, Josh thought that perhaps it wouldn't matter, that his little adventure would be overlooked in the day-to-day busyness of the school and nobody would ever discover what had happened. He certainly wasn't going to rush into a foolhardy confession just because of a chance visit ten minutes after the crime. He mustered a smile that he hoped looked natural and flung the door open.

"Come in, sir," he said quietly.

Instead of walking into the room immediately like he had done at other times, the Master stood on the threshold and gave him a searching smile. Josh's heart dropped. He knew. He must know, and even if he didn't already, those searching eyes could see right through him and notice the black stain on his conscience. He flushed slightly and fought the urge to confess everything and beg for mercy. Then again, what difference would it make? Even the Master couldn't undo what he had done. Now that the creature was gone, the only thing confessing would do would be to prove him unworthy of belonging to the castle, and there was nothing he wanted more than to stay where he was forever. He waited patiently for the Master to speak, and after what seemed like an interminable time, he finally broke the silence.

"I came to tell you that you have been selected to go on patrol tomorrow," he said quietly.

Josh grinned happily. He had been waiting for this honour for a long time. Each week there were one or two freshmen chosen to accompany the knights of the castle on the week-long patrol. It was adventurous, a little bit dangerous, and only the top students were chosen to go. Besides, it was an entire week spent outside the confines of the castle and the grounds, something that appealed to Josh's active nature. Thank goodness he hadn't ruined his chance by confessing what he had done!

"That's great," he said enthusiastically. "I thought my turn would never come."

The Master smiled at him again and seemed to wait. Josh became uncomfortable and wondered if perhaps he really did know what had happened and was merely testing him. It was too risky to say anything then. If he still felt that he needed to confess everything, he could do it after he got back.

"Well, you'd better get a good night's rest. The patrol is long and tiring and it wouldn't be a good idea to start off tired," he said softly and turned away from the door.

"Thank you," Josh said, feeling vaguely disappointed that there hadn't been more to the visit as he watched the Master walk away. He still had to fight the urge to rush after him and tell him everything. Instead, he firmly closed the door to his room, determined that absolutely nothing would jeopardize his chance to go on patrol.

It was a sleepless night after all. Every time he closed his eyes, the image of the glowing red glare of the monster stared back at him. He tossed and turned, sure that the sound of the wind howling around the castle turrets and the beating rain on the window were the sounds of the creature returning to vent its rage on him. Morning found him early—wan and tired with dark circles under his eyes.

As he quickly dressed in the dark he suddenly remembered that during the week of patrol the knights slept outside. What if the creature came in the night to where they were camped? There would be no walls or closed windows to save him then. Suddenly the adventure that he had anticipated so eagerly took on an unexpectedly sinister aspect that buried his excitement in fear.

It was cold, and a drizzling misty rain fell from clouds that seemed to hang just a few feet above the trees of the forest. When Josh finally made his appearance, the rest of the knights were already mounted and ready. A horse was held in waiting for him by one of the stable workers and he mounted awkwardly, weighed down with his pack and the light armour that all the trainees wore. Most of the field work his class had done had been on foot and he had only the most basic experience with horses. However, he felt confident of his ability to learn quickly and held the reins with pretended nonchalance as he took his place near the back of the line.

When the captain finally emerged from the castle, Josh was surprised to see him in deep consultation with the Master, who was walking along beside him. The two of them paused to look in his direction and he had the uncomfortable feeling that they were talking about him. With a pang of guilt, his conscience reminded him that he really did not deserve to go along with the patrol. Stubbornly, he pushed the thought back, convinced that confessing his disobedience would do nothing but get him into trouble.

The Master walked with the captain all the way to his horse and then waited while he mounted and the captain made some sort of final remonstrance that Josh could not hear. What he did overhear was the reply of the Master, who fixed a thoughtful gaze on his young student and, in a tone of voice that made no further room for argument, said, "Nevertheless, he goes along, in spite of the risk."

Josh felt a wave of fear, remembering that somewhere in the forest was an evil that he was responsible for releasing and nobody knew about it. He wondered if there was yet another danger that they were afraid would put him in harm's way. None of the other students had faced very much risk, but this strange discussion made him feel even more nervous.

Riding with the patrol was usually a routine exercise. The knights who rode were accomplished fighters, but they circulated through the Master's country mostly to maintain the peace and prevent encroachments by the enemy rather than having to fight the kinds of battles that won the kingdom in the first place. Those battles that were still being fought were on more distant ground. The few times there had been an altercation closer to home, the battles had been easily won by the Master and his knights.

He shivered as he remembered the overwhelming terror inspired by the creature. The prisoners brought in by the patrol were generally of the creeping reptilian type—servants of the enemy indeed, but nothing much to fear as far as he could tell.

Now again was a final chance to tell the Master about what had happened the night before. Perhaps the safety of the whole patrol was at risk because of him. It would be a week before he would see the Master again, but he had pushed the urge to confess everything down enough times by then that it was becoming an easier thing to do. He rationalized the urge away, telling himself that it could make no difference. What was done was done. The knights of the patrol were warriors, and if they did encounter the creature, they should be able to defeat it. The Master must have guessed that he would have been curious about the forbidden room. If he had really wanted the creature to remain in its prison, it was a foolish decision to put a boy in the room below. On a certain level, he decided, it was really the Master's fault that the creature had escaped at all.

Then the moment was over and they rode out of the courtyard with clattering hooves and jingling bridles. Josh saw the Master watching him as he rode past and tried to smile brightly as he waved goodbye. As the forest canopy closed over his head, he was gripped with the excitement of riding with the patrol and felt that he had made the right decision about telling the Master the truth. There would be time to do that after his week of adventure was over. He glanced back and saw the closed gate of the castle framed by the tunnel of the forest pathway. He could almost forget the grey clouds and the chilly rain as he absorbed the smells of wet pine, damp earthy greenery, and steaming horses. Occasionally he caught glimpses of birds, squirrels, and rabbits as they flitted off the path ahead of the column. He sat as steadily as he could, trying to mimic the riders ahead of him as the horse jogged obediently along in line. It was tempting to urge the animal into a gallop and fly off into the wilderness with an exuberant whoop.

After a while, his excitement settled down into the monotony of familiarity. Josh passed through places that he remembered from his journey to the Master. In those days, the forest had seemed like a fearful place full of lurking shadows and whispered threats. Now, in company with the king's soldiers, he saw it for what it was: a place of beauty and peace. It was part of the Master's domain and belonged to him.

They camped that night on the edge of the forest, where they were sheltered somewhat from the weather by the spreading boughs. The next day they would begin the part of the patrol that would take them into more populated places, where they would search for those who had heard the Master's Music and needed help on their journey. While there, they would also watch for signs that the evil one had made inroads against the Master's land.

Josh remembered how the common people spoke of the knights of the Master and how fear drove them at times to attack the very ones who were sent to protect them. He thought of the patrol that had helped him on his journey toward the music and how, at first, not understanding their intentions and still convinced of the truth of the superstitious stories that he had heard, he had tried to run away from them. They had kept him on the right path at that time and shortened the road considerably, but there had been the fear to overcome first.

The common people, until they chose to listen to the music of the Master, were unable to appreciate his servants or even understand that the vague rumours and dreadful atrocities assigned to those who rode under the banner of the music were completely foreign to their natures. Only those who had followed the call knew the truth behind the patrols and the knights that rode on them. For the rest, the good deeds that were done were tempered by the fear inspired by the myths they had heard, leading only to more confusion, rumour, and conjecture.

During the night, Josh awoke to the sound of a murmured warning from the knight that stood guard at the edge of the camp. A feeling of cold terror swept over him like the shadow of a cloud crossing the sun. He peered up through the dark trees and thought, with a shiver, that he could perceive a place of deeper darkness. Even as he thought he had picked it out of the surrounding night, it shifted like the mist and was gone. For a brief instant before it disappeared, he was sure he saw the red glow of the creature's eyes glaring down at them. In that second he was prepared to shriek out a warning to the others, but then the thing had melted into the night in such a way that he could not be sure that what he thought he had seen was real at all. A faint shriek of malice seemed to echo out of the dark and twist around the camp for an instant, but even that could have been the product of his terrified imagination. He couldn't be sure enough to risk saying anything. Instead, he spent the rest of the night in wakeful watchfulness, tensely waiting for it to return and be palpable enough for him to raise an alarm against it. Finally, he saw the darkness of the cloudy night melt into the grey mist of a damp morning, and he closed his eyes for the short hour before it was time to wake up.

That day the route took them deep into the farmland and he had to endure the suspicious stares of the farmers and their families as they rode along the road. They were not welcomed in any way, but at the same time, nobody was overtly hostile either.

It surprised him, then, when that afternoon the group was approached by a distraught farmer who rushed in their direction when he saw them coming. He waved frantically in the direction of his fields and started shouting his story long before he was close enough to be heard. Josh stared at the man's terror-stricken face as he stumbled over his description of the monster that had attacked him. He groaned inwardly as the group directed their horses off the main road and his mind whispered that he was about to meet the creature of his nightmares. He still hoped he wouldn't have to say anything about the attic, but if the monster the man was describing did turn out to be the same creature, he would have to speak up. As they picked their way slowly through the muddy ruts, he clung to the faintest of hopes that there would be something to interrupt their progress before he had to face what he now knew to be the inevitable disclosure of the truth.

After what seemed like a very long time, they came to a small strip of woodland that separated the farmer's land into two fields. The farmer hung back fearfully as he told them that the thing had disappeared into the trees at the far end of the field and they would see what it had done for themselves if they went to where his abandoned plough lay awkwardly on its side. From the back of the line, Josh peered nervously through the thin brush into the field. At first he could see nothing but the thick, muddy furrows left by the plough. Then he saw the horse lying next to the plough and a wave of nausea swept over him.

The riders cautiously approached the motionless animal while the farmer, clinging closely to them, described the great dark monster that had come out of the sky and attacked them at their work. As they approached, Josh looked away, afraid that he was going to be sick at his first sight of a violent death. The horse lay stretched awkwardly on the ground with its head twisted at an angle that it could never have achieved in life. The ground beneath was saturated with the darkness of the blood that had poured out of the gaping wound where the flesh had been torn out of its throat. It had occurred so suddenly that there had not even been a struggle for life before death found it.

Several of the knights dismounted and helped the farmer untangle the horse from the harness while a few others set about digging a grave for the poor animal. The rest remained mounted on their horses and made a slow search around the perimeter of the field for any further signs of the creature. There was nothing to be found and they returned after their fruitless exploration to reassure the farmer as much as they could. One of the knights remained behind to continue the investigation and offer a semblance of protection for the family. He would return to the Master on his own in a day or two and give a full report.

After the incident, Josh saw nothing further that made him suspect that the creature was anywhere around for the rest of the week. He began to hope that he had seen the last of it and that the event could be passed over as he had planned in the beginning. He hadn't considered his own conscience, however, and found that the struggle with his own feelings of guilt grew even stronger than the fear that he had felt in the presence of the shadow. He did everything that he could to ignore the nagging knowledge that he was responsible for the death of the farmer's horse and who knew what other calamities. He imagined all sorts of horrible things as he rode along with the knights. It turned the adventure that he had longed for and worked so hard to achieve into a chore that he couldn't wait to finish. Every encounter they had with the people set him on edge as he anxiously waited for more news of the shadow creature.

They returned to the castle late on the seventh day. The captain left his horse in the care of one of the grooms as soon as they entered and immediately went inside to make his report. The rest of the knights took responsibility for the care of their own horses, and Josh was exhausted when he finally found himself back in his own room. Wearily, he dropped his pack on the floor, shed the light armour that over the last couple of days had grown more and more heavy, and made his way towards the bed, longing only for a good long rest and the ease of stretching his aching body out on the soft mattress. An urgent knock at his door stopped him abruptly, and he reluctantly turned away from his inviting bed to open the door.

One of the knights from the patrol was waiting for him in the hall.

"The Master wants you," he said briefly, without smiling, and then waited to accompany the tired boy to the Master's chambers.

Josh felt a sudden pang of fear and guilt as he trudged along beside the knight. Was he about to be accused of his misdemeanour and the additional crime of hiding it? What if the Master had investigated the attic in his absence and discovered that the shadow was missing? What would happen to him then? Would he be sent away in disgrace? His face flushed with the shame of that thought. He could imagine the scene of his return to his family. He could almost hear the "I told you so" and the derisive laughter of his brothers and father as they mocked his foolish failure. His mother wouldn't laugh at him, but he knew that the look of disappointment in her eyes would be the hardest to bear of all. After all, she was the one who had encouraged him to follow the music in the first place, even though she couldn't hear it. She had never heard the music, but she believed in the stories and hoped that someday, if he followed the dream to the end, he would return and teach her.

The heavy doors of the Master's room swung open to admit them as soon as they knocked. Josh glanced nervously around the room and noted that most of the members of the patrol were present and stood along the walls, waiting. The Master sat on his throne and Josh thought his face looked more disturbed than he had ever seen it. His heart thudded fearfully as he approached the seat that had always been a place of comfort and joy until today. He hated that he did not want to meet the loving eyes and carefully avoided the searching gaze that he knew could look deep into his heart and read what was hiding there. He studied the floor and the ceiling and the heavy tapestries that surrounded the room; he even fixed his gaze on the Master's feet, but he would not look into his eyes.

"Josh, I have asked each of my knights what they saw and experienced on the patrol this week. There has been a disturbing report from your leader, and I am trying to gather any evidence that you can offer me."

Josh hesitated for an instant and suddenly realized that it was too late to tell the truth. After all his delays and excuses, he had missed his chance. In a faltering voice, he told only the story of what he had seen in the farmer's field. When he was finished speaking, the Master waited for a long time without saying anything. Curiously, Josh ventured a look into his eyes, but he could stand only a very quick glance at the mingled pain, love, and compassion he saw there.

"Josh..." he finally said softly, in a voice that pulled at the boy's heart until he wanted to fling himself in a tearful heap at his feet. "This has been an upsetting thing for you, hasn't it?"

He was about to respond when the door burst open and a dishevelled knight rushed in. Josh recognized him as the captain of another group and stared in wonder at the obvious distress in his face. It almost looked like he was afraid!

"What is it?" the Master asked calmly, seeming to forget Josh for the moment.

"There is a fiend on the loose!" the knight burst out. "Our patrol discovered him in the mountains several days ago when the fleeing villagers met us on the road. The creature seems to have settled there and has spent its time since disembowelling the livestock and throwing boulders into the fields and at houses until the people have grown so afraid that they've run away from it. They've left everything behind and are starving on the road now. You know how much trouble one of these creatures can be! I thought we had captured all of them, but..."

"Perhaps one has escaped," the Master said quietly.

It was too much! It didn't matter what shame or disgrace he fell into. He had a responsibility to tell the truth and he was almost certain that the Master knew all about it anyway. He knew everything and had known right from the beginning. It was suddenly so clear that there was nothing hidden and Josh's stupid attempt to conceal what he had done had only made things worse. With a crimson face and a ragged sob of relief, he threw himself on the floor in front of the Master. The story poured out of him, and when he finished telling it, he waited for the anger to fall. Instead, he heard the quiet footsteps of the knights as one by one they filed wordlessly out of the council chambers, leaving him alone with the Master.

When they were gone, the Master finally spoke.

"Josh . . ."

His voice was gentle and Josh started to weep again. It was so absolutely unexpected to find that the Master still loved him. All the defences he had built up to protect himself against the wrath he had expected dissolved into tearful devotion. It didn't matter that every knight in the patrol had witnessed his shame. What mattered was that he still belonged.

With gentle hands, the Master raised him to his feet and pulled him into an embrace that spoke the forgiveness and mercy that was in his heart.

"You would have been better to have told me from the beginning. It would have been so much easier for you."

When his tears finally subsided, the Master led him out of the chambers and back to his room.

"You need to rest," he told him gently. "There will be much for you to do tomorrow. There is the task of restoration ahead, and I'll warn you now, it will not be an easy one."

Josh nodded wearily and impulsively grasped the Master's hand in a grateful squeeze before he opened the door of his room. He saw the promise of help in his eyes and realized afresh how he had compounded mistake upon mistake by refusing to admit what he had done.

They left the castle early the next morning and rode hard all day through forest and then farmland until they had to slow down to make way for the streams of refugees that were walking in the opposite direction. Josh wanted to burst into tears when he saw the look of lost desolation on their faces as they made their journey, with all their worldly goods minimized to what could be pushed in a wheelbarrow or carried on their backs. Everything that was happening to them was his fault. After awhile, he couldn't stand to look any longer and instead focused his attention on the golden armour of the Master, who led the way.

Occasionally, as they carefully picked their way through the hoards, one of the refugees would shout at them. Sometimes they begged for food. Sometimes they threw bitter accusations at the knights who had failed to protect them, ignoring the fact that they were obviously heading in the direction that must lead to a battle. No matter what the cry, the Master paused every time and gave them a few words of loving reassurance before they went any further.

Josh chafed a little bit at each delay, annoyed at the patience of someone who seemed to have all the time in the world to speak to each and every person that bothered to address him. All he wanted to do was to get the ordeal over with as quickly as possible. His fear of encountering the creature in battle had evaporated the morning they left, as soon as he had seen the Master emerge from the castle, dressed in his own armour and prepared to accompany him on the journey. The first part had even taken on a sense of festivity as they rode together and talked. Not that all their talk had been easy. Josh had many lessons to learn and the process was being expedited by necessity. Even their slow, patient progress through the crowd of desperate people was one of those soul-changing lessons that he only began to learn on that road. However, the closer they came to the final crisis, the more nervous he became, and each delay only made things worse.

As if he sensed Josh's frustration, the Master turned an occasional loving smile in his direction and he was encouraged to keep his horse plodding slowly along no matter what his own ideas about rushing into the battle might be.

They finally found the fiend, grown to gigantic proportions after feeding its rage for over a week, clinging to the edge of a cliff that overhung a small village and its surrounding farms. As they approached, it suddenly seized a boulder the size of a small cow and sent it catapulting through the air into the middle of a field, where it cut a swath of destruction several hundred yards long.

As all his horror of the creature swiftly returned, Josh glanced at the Master, hoping for a renewal of the confidence that he had felt when they started out. The Master sat quietly next to him and met his gaze with an encouraging smile and a slight nod. "Not enough!" Josh thought as he took a deep breath, hating that it trembled. He settled himself firmly in the saddle and drew his sword with an arm that now felt weak and shaky. It was not nearly enough, but with the Master there watching his every move, there was nothing else for him to do but ride forward. At least his death would be quick if he were struck by one of those fly boulders! Instead of throwing any more rocks, the creature suddenly let go of its perch and soared into the sky on wings that seemed to cast a shadow over the whole world.

It gave an ear-splitting shriek that numbed Josh's mind with fear even as he tried to focus on the task at hand and plan where to strike when the time should come. He didn't think he would get more than one chance at it and he meant to make the best effort he could. An instant later, a searing pain went through his shoulder and he was lying on the ground—sword-less, breathless, and at the mercy of the enemy that was now hovering menacingly directly above him. Josh staggered to his feet and stared helplessly at this thing that he now had no idea how to defeat. He thought about the dead horse they had seen on patrol and shuddered inwardly at the thought of his own blood spilled out into the field where he stood. The fiend floated leisurely toward him. Sure of its prey, it no longer hurried, and the red eyes crinkled in malevolent silent laughter as it came. Josh closed his eyes and waited for the inevitable, when suddenly he felt a hand on his shoulder drawing him back.

"It is enough," the voice of the Master said softly but so firmly that the fiend stopped in its advance and hissed furiously.

The Master gently pulled Josh back until he stood behind him, and Josh could see with a shock that the Master had removed his armour. Filled with fear that was no longer on his own behalf, Josh tried to push his beloved teacher out of harm's way, but it was too late. The creature pounced and then retreated with a shriek of agony as it was literally consumed before their eyes. As the blackness disappeared, Josh turned with a grin of triumph to the Master, only to encounter his anguished expression. A gaping wound in his neck told the story that the death of the creature had not come without great cost.

He assisted his wounded teacher back to the horses and helped him bandage the wound. The Master painfully resumed his armour and they mounted their horses for the return journey.

As they traveled, they told everyone that they met that the fiend was dead and that it was safe again to return to their homes. To Josh's surprise, the news was greeted by a mixture of disbelief and suspicion, although many of the refugees were eventually convinced to at least go and see. Once they were finally in the forest again and the stream of people had thinned out so they could have some privacy, Josh could restrain his questions no longer.

"I don't understand how you destroyed the creature!" he finally exclaimed.

The Master gave him a smile that was half grimace because of the pain.

"Well, you can't battle the greatest evil. The only way to destroy great evil is to fight it with a greater good. The greatest love in the world happens when one person is truly willing to sacrifice their life for another, especially when that other person doesn't deserve it at all. I love you enough to die for you even though you did the wrong thing when you disobeyed my request to leave the attic closed. The instant the fiend tasted pure love, it died."

Josh stared tearfully at the face of the one who had given him every ounce of his love, unable to find words enough to say thank you.

"Did you know when you did it? I mean…well, were you sure it would work?"

The Master chuckled softly, "It was a theory, and I have to admit that testing it hasn't been the most comfortable experience."

Once again Josh looked away, searching for expression until he finally found what he wanted to say.

"You have my life."

TWILA SLID HER HAND around the Master's neck and gently laid her fingers on the jagged scar that remained. Her eyes filled as she thought about the love that he had shown Josh. Then it was as if knowledge flowed from that scar into her mind, flooding her with the conviction of its truth.

"You would do that for any one of us," she gasped as the amazing thought swept over her.

His own eyes were wet as he gazed at each one of them in turn. "Yes, I would," he said without hesitation.

"You could have been killed!" Marcus exclaimed.

"Yes, but that was not the most important thing at the time. I trusted that I would not be killed, even though it was a very real possibility."

Twila quickly kissed the shoulder she had been leaning on. "You have my life," she said softly.

"I can't believe that I ever doubted you," she commented after a short pause.

"You're not the first and you won't be the last to doubt. The music calls with the truth, but even here the truth can be mislaid. You know that. Wisdom grows; it is not born suddenly. Where a lesson has been truly learned, there is no need to go back and relearn it again."

The Master gave her a hug and then rose from the sofa. His visit was over and it was with a sort of satisfied longing that they each wished him goodnight.

When he was gone, Marie turned to the young girl who was now next to her. "It sounds as if you've been learning the difficult lessons too," she said with a softness that was unusual for her.

Twila flushed and looked into the fire with some embarrassment. "I still can't believe how very foolish I was, but since you've all shared a story, I'm willing to tell you mine if you want to hear it," she said shyly. She was, after all, the youngest member of their little party and still a novice.

"I think that we would all love to hear about what you and the Master have been working so hard on together," Marie encouraged her, and the others nodded in eager agreement. It was far too early to go to bed and it was so comfortable together in their cosy corner by the fireplace.

The girl who, up until so recently, had known so little kindness or acceptance, for the first time opened up her heart to tell part of her story to her new family.

Twila

I CAME ALONE. My father disappeared when I was a baby, and when Mother died there was nothing left for me, so I wandered from one place and person to another until the music gave me a direction to walk in. Then I found the castle and met the Master.

He handled me gently at first. Alone and afraid, I was as timid as a lost fawn: unsure, nervous, and doubtful of everything good that I saw. If he had been anything but what he was at the beginning, I believe I would have bolted and been lost forever, but he was much wiser than that. A soft voice followed me and words of love wooed me into a place of confidence and security. In a mood of grateful joy at having at last found home, I wandered through this rich house and the gardens uninhibited by fear for the first time I could remember. There was no one to condemn me. No one said I must or must not, and I respected all that I saw and touched out of the love I found growing in my heart for him.

I wanted to please, to impress, to return a portion of what he had given me. I went to him with the matter on my lips and pressed him for a task. Oh, the wonder of his smile at that moment! I felt as if the desire to please him alone had pleased him more than anything else I could have done. His eyes lit with love and he gave me work to do. I was happy about that. I had thought at first that it would be difficult to persuade him to let me work for him, but it was as if he had anticipated me in even this desire and had prepared a suitable occupation in advance. It was just such a thing as I would have chosen for myself.

At first I set about the work with great eagerness. What a joy it was to feel that I was serving him in any small way. There were difficulties, of course, but I was able to get through them, and afterwards, they seemed as if they were nothing. Then I found that the task was greater than I'd first thought. The difficulties became larger and the work began to consume me. I spent long hours struggling with it, and when I was not working my mind continually returned to the problems that arose every day.

I became a stranger to the gardens and the beautiful galleries. I rarely saw him anymore, and when we did meet I found that my unfinished task loomed between us—an unspoken question and an unsatisfactory reply. He never asked about it and I never told him how I struggled with it. If I could not even do this thing for him, how could I retain his love? So there it stood, a wall that took my time and stilted our once-animated conversations.

As I struggled further, I found that I began to harbour seeds of doubt about his love. If he loved me so much, why would he assign me to such a difficult task? Did he want me busy and out of the way so he could pursue his own activities without my interruptions? Did he want me to fail for some reason? Did he love me at all or was I simply an instrument to be used in his service? As more and more questions rose in my mind and grew without answers, I found resentment, bitterness, and yes, even hatred in my heart.

He never looked in on me to see how I did. (At least not that I noticed.) My anger grew along with the difficulties of my work and I began to avoid encounters with him. I blamed him for it all and I shrank into an angry, timid creature once again.

Finally, one day I threw my hands up in despair and kicked the thing aside. I was determined to work no longer and I was going to leave. I would walk out and find my own way. I could remember nothing before that was any worse than this, and back then I did not also have the pain of disappointment lingering on every moment of the day. I found him standing outside the door of the room when I furiously threw it open.

"Where are you going?" he asked quietly as I tried to brush past him.

Without giving him an answer, I hurtled myself back into the room, slammed the door in his face, and turned back to my work. I thought then that he was standing guard to make sure that I did what I was told. He must have known how difficult the task would become and that I would eventually try to escape from it. I had become a slave! A prisoner! A captive assigned to the never ending, impossible task of the ogre king in the fairytales my mother used to tell me. It was a fate worse than any other I could have imagined. For a while he knocked at the door, but I was too angry to answer. Then he left me alone again and I returned to what I realized was a futile waste of time and not a job at all.

After that day it seemed I met him more and more often in the halls when I made my way to the dining room or to my quarters. I would pass by him most of the time without a word. He could keep me a prisoner, but I wasn't going to pretend that I was happy about it. Sometimes he even spoke gently to me and my heart would leap at the sound before I could stop it and remind myself of what he had done to me. I never once actually looked to see if there was any hurt in his face. I never considered his feelings at all.

He was patient. Never angry, never demanding, but always present. I knew that he was often just outside the door during the day. At night I could hear him pacing the halls or back and forth in his rooms that are directly above my own. Sometimes I would think about the early days and long for their return. Sometimes I wondered why he did not allow me to leave or at least become angry enough at my constant snubs to throw me out. After all, he was the one who held all of the power. We had reached an impasse and I dwelt in my solitude, wishing, in spite of my anger, for a return to the days of our friendship.

I finally reached the end of my endurance one morning. I walked into my work room and began to wreck everything. Anything I could tear off I did. I kicked it until parts of it broke. I screamed at it as if it were alive and could be hurt by my words. I tried to kill it by every means in my power as if it were a thing that could be killed. I never heard him enter the room, but suddenly his arms were around me, holding and subduing. My rage melted away, leaving the tears of frustration and failure.

"You left me alone," I accused him as I struggled to get away.

"You were never alone," he answered, holding on even more tightly.

"I can't do this. I cannot do what you asked me to do!"

"No, you can't. I know that you can't do it."

"Then why did you give it to me?" I asked through gritted teeth as his statement sunk in and I became angry all over again.

"Because I wanted to do it together; I wanted to teach and guide and help you to achieve."

"Where have you been, then?"

"Outside the door, waiting."

"I knew it! You were watching me. Why didn't you just come in and help me?"

"Because you never asked."

I remember how my anger drained away when he said that. Right away I could see what an idiot I had been, and I was ashamed of myself. I wanted him to be angry with me, but of course he wasn't. Instead, he walked over to the mess I had made and started picking up the pieces.

"So can I finally help you with this?" he asked, with one of those dear eyebrows raised over eyes that twinkled with just a hint of laughter.

There was nothing left to do then but go help clean it up and see what we could salvage. Before we were finished we were both laughing like crazy kids and everything was beautiful between us again. We've been working together on it ever since.

 "And just what is 'it'?" Marie asked archly.

Twila smiled secretively.

"That I can't tell you, but rest assured that the task is coming along very well, and one day soon all will be revealed."

"Anything the Master put his hand to will certainly be worth seeing," Timothy commented eagerly.

"Or hearing…" Marie added as she searched Twila's face for any reaction that might be a clue about the mysterious project.

Twila laughed again. "It's getting very late now and I must go before I give anything away."

She jumped up quickly, then paused.

"Thank you," she said. "I learned a lot tonight and I'm glad."

"We did too," Marie smiled. "Good night, dear."

Twila received the "dear"-ing without her usual hint of resentment. It didn't sound condescending to her anymore. Instead, she gave the older woman a quick hug and fled the room before she could cry.

"She's got a beautiful song," Timothy commented approvingly as the door closed behind her.

"We all have beautiful songs now," Marie replied.

Printed in the United States
140294LV00004B/3/P